A YEAR TO REMEMBER

A YEAR TO REMEMBER

a Reminiscence of 1931

Alec Waugh

W. H. ALLEN · LONDON
A division of Howard & Wyndham Ltd
1975

Printed and bound in Great Britain by
W & J Mackay Limited, Chatham,
for the publishers, W. H. Allen & Co. Ltd,
44 Hill Street, London W1X 8LB

ISBN 0 491 01564 X

ALEC WAUGH
has written almost fifty books. They include:

Novels
The Loom of Youth (1917)
Kept (1925)
So Lovers Dream (1931)
Wheels within Wheels (1933)
The Balliols (1934)
Jill Somerset (1936)
No Truce with Time (1941)
Unclouded Summer (1948)
Guy Renton (1953)
Island in the Sun (1956)
Fuel for the Flame (1960)
The Mule on the Minaret (1965)
A Spy in the Family (1970)
The Fatal Gift (1973)

Short Stories
My Place in the Bazaar (1961)

Travel
Hot Countries (1930)
The Sugar Islands (1958)

Autobiographies
The Early Years of Alec Waugh (1962)
My Brother Evelyn and Other Portraits (1967)

Miscellaneous
In Praise of Wine (1959)
A Family of Islands (1964)
Wines and Spirits (Time-Life Books; 1968)
Bangkok: The Story of a City (1970)

I

One lives in the past when one is over seventy, and I was born in July 1898.

At the M.C.C. dinner in 1969, I asked E. W. Swanton if he would like me to write an article for *The Cricketer* on the fiftieth anniversary of Plum Warner's last match at Lord's. I was a keen Middlesex supporter, and for such a one as myself, August 1920 was a desperately exciting month. To everyone's astonishment, Middlesex had won nine matches in succession and on August 28th stood at the head of the table, but they had to win their last game against Surrey to carry off the championship. The last day was one of the most dramatic that Lord's has ever seen. When it started, the betting against a Middlesex victory was a hundred to one, at least. But by twenty past six it was all over, and the crowd was streaming across the ground, with Warner carried shoulder high to the Pavilion.

I finished my piece by saying, 'All that is half a century ago. During that half century I have had a whole lot of fun and I am still ticking over, but there is no single day that I would sooner live again than August 31st 1920.'

I entitled the article *The day that I'd soonest relive*, and after I had mailed it I began to wonder which whole year I would soonest live again. To my surprise I found myself selecting 1931.

I say 'to my surprise' because in synopsis it may well seem unexceptional. At its start I was a bachelor of thirty-two, living in a rented furnished apartment in New York, about to start a lecture tour. When it was over, a bachelor still, I was in mid-Atlantic on my way back to New York. At that period of my life I was constantly making ambitious trips to the Far East, the South Seas, the West Indies. But 1931 was geographically unadventurous. I returned to England at the end of March. After a few days in London, I spent ten weeks in the South of France, mainly at Villefranche. I was back in England at the end of June, but by mid-July I was again in Villefranche. This time, though, only for two weeks. The rest of the year I spent in England.

It was an industrious year. During January and February, I finished a novel that I had begun in England in October. In Villefranche I wrote in its entirety a novel that was published in England in November with the title *So Lovers Dream* and in the U.S.A. in January as *That American Woman*; the original version was 140,000 words long.

In the autumn the London publishing house of Benn sponsored a series of short (40,000 word) novels, paper covered, at 9d each. I adapted a newspaper serial as my contribution. At the end of the year, I assembled, under the title *Thirteen Such Years*, a miscellany of sketches, portraits and short stories, that attempted to present a picture of England between 1918 and 1931. I wrote several articles and half a dozen short stories. I must have written a quarter of a million words. They were on the whole well enough received. I enjoyed the writing of *So Lovers Dream* more than I had that of any novel since my first, and a few months ago it was reissued in a hard back edition.

For me as a writer, the tides were then flowing hopefully. A pound bought six times what it does today. I was paying £225 a year for a four-roomed flat in Chelsea. Cassell's paid me an advance of £600 a novel. In the U.S.A. I usually got $1000. Travel books brought in about £250 on each side; a short story in England – Nash's was my best market – earned £40. In the U.S.A. – not having yet achieved the 'glossies' – I was happy to get $150 from *Harper's Bazaar*. But I did not always, by any means, sell my short stories in the U.S.A. Newspaper articles fetched £10 to £15 a piece. I was making some £1,600 a year. I was always slightly in debt, but not uncomfortably, provided I did not spend too much time in London.

My friends used to wonder how I could afford to do so much travelling. But actually travel was an economy for me. I did not have to indulge in costly entertaining. My social life was provided by the ships in which I travelled, and in the islands that I visited I was a guest more often than a host. I never during 1931 had a substantial credit balance at my bank; more than once I received one of those notes so typical of English banking, 'Your account appears to be overdrawn £23. 11. 6. We shall be glad to receive your instructions in this matter.' But I was never insolvent.

At the same time I did not receive a single one of those surprises that make authorship so constant an adventure. Hilaire Belloc wrote of that dream of us all, 'the return of lost loves and great wads of unexpected wealth' and how often is not a writer enlivened and encouraged, 'restored to life and power and thought' by a cable or a telephone call announcing a serial, book club, paperback or film sale. Not a single such cable came to me in 1931. It was as undramatic a year professionally as it had been an unadventurous year geographically.

And in romance, too, it was unremarkable. There was no 'soul shattering' experience; instead there were two delightful passages, one in New York and one in Villefranche. I call them 'passages' rather than 'passades' because my two partners remained in my life; we separated but did not part. With the Villefranche friend I was in touch until her death, four years ago, with the last letter that I had written her returned unopened. Both of them came to mean much more to me than at the start I had suspected that they would. But I did not guess that then. It might indeed seem that 1931 was for me a year in which very little happened, rather like the calm in the centre of a typhoon. But it did not seem like that at the time nor does it now in retrospect. It has on the contrary a very special quality of sustained variety, of anticipation and fulfilment. Most things went right; hardly anything went wrong.

A few years ago I published a partial autobiography called *The Early Years of Alec Waugh*. It closed in June 1930, a few weeks before my thirty-second birthday. I had reached, I said, a watershed. A love affair with a married woman, Ruth, a Californian, round which, for three years, my plans had been arranged, had just come to a close. I had travelled many thousand miles on her account. Now my long bondage was at an end. At the same time a new life had started for me in New York. My travel book *Hot Countries* had been chosen by an American book club, the Literary Guild, and I had been fêted in Manhattan in the manner traditional for such spoilt beneficiaries of fortune.

3

My early novels had all of them been published in America; one of them, a story called *Kept* about post-war London, had not sold badly, but I had had scarcely any personal contacts there. The publicity that attended the launching of *Hot Countries* made me in a small way a New York personality. Colston Leigh, just starting as a lecture agent, was ready to finance a tour for me.

June 1930 was a good point at which to stop the first part of an autobiography, with some things ending, with other things beginning. Yet a watershed is more than a railway station where you change trains. The Random House Dictionary's first definition of the word is 'the ridge or crest line dividing two drainage areas'. Its third definition is 'a point of division as between two periods of history'. It has, that is to say, dimensions; it has a terrain, a climate, a foliage of its own; and, as I thought of what it had been for me, I realised that for the modern world, too, it had been a watershed. 1930 marked the end of the post-war period. 1932 was the start of the pre-war period. 1931 was a no man's land and I felt that there would be a point in reliving that year on paper in terms of what was happening both to me and to my friends and to the world around us. I hoped, too, it might be of interest to record the problems and activities of a professional writer during a single year. I had no source of income other than the earnings of my pen.

In 1966 I was installed as a writer in residence at Central State College, Edmond, Oklahoma, to teach 'creative writing'. In my opening address I warned my students that creative writing could not be taught; the most I could do was to tell them what being a professional writer meant. And so in the course of two semesters I explained to them the problems that I had been set by the forty-odd books that I had written, with each book setting its own special problem. I told them that they could learn as much for the purpose of their own writing from studying the mistakes that a professional writer has made as from examining the technique by which a master has achieved his effects, and seen in that light the various projects that I undertook during 1931 contain useful examples of the pitfalls that befall a writer along his way. One cannot be taught how to write. One teaches oneself by writing.

There is another reason why I am yielding to an impulse to

write about 1931. In the following year I married. The marriage produced three children. I do not believe that it is possible to write the complete truth about a marriage that has produced children.

II

1931 began for me in a New York flat to which Muriel Draper had invited a number of friends to see a bad year out. Muriel Draper, the sister of Ruth Draper, was one of the more vivid ornaments of the New York scene. For days afterwards I heard anecdotes of what had happened there later in the morning; it was undoubtedly an historic party, as most of Muriel Draper's were, but I was not present to assess the veracity of those rumours. I left soon after twelve because next morning I was due at Albany to hear Franklin D. Roosevelt deliver his inaugural address to the State Assembly as the re-elected Governor of New York State. The train left early. I wanted to feel well and rested. There would be other wild parties in New York, and I was not likely to be invited again to a gubernatorial opening.

In the apartment house in which I lived, 136 E 36 – a building on the corner of Lexington which still stands – was also living an assemblyman, Langdon Post. I had arranged to go down with him to Albany. I knocked on his door at five o'clock. He clearly had not been as cautious as I had the night before. I had to knock a number of times and I doubt if I should have succeeded in rousing him if I had not had the co-operation of his dog. He was under thirty, but he looked over forty when he eventually peered round the door. His eyes were half closed and his chin was bristly. Electric razors did not exist in those days. I assumed that he would arrive at the station with either a lacerated or a half-shaven jaw.

He arrived with both. Others were in his plight. The railroad coach was filled with, I presumed, distinguished citizens. They did not look as though they were. They resembled an army in retreat that has flung away its packs and rifles. Most of them slumped into slumber the moment they were stretched out on a seat. Two hours later, when a sandwich man came round with coffee and doughnuts, they fought their way back to consciousness. Some of them, I supposed, were members of the State Assembly.

Others were notables whom Roosevelt had invited for the buffet barbecue that would follow the inauguration ceremony. They did not lack powers of recovery, for at the subsequent reception I did not notice anyone with a haggard or dishevelled look.

My presence in Albany was due to the fact that in the previous summer I had brought out from England a letter of introduction to Eleanor Roosevelt from Lady Willert, the wife of Sir Arthur Willert, who, during the war as *The Times'* representative in New York, had been able to perform several important intelligence operations for the government; for these he had been knighted. He was now press attaché to the Foreign Office.

It has been often remarked that the *arriviste* can get farther in three days in a foreign country if he is provided with the right letters of introduction than he can in three years in the country of his birth. On the strength of that letter I was during the summer invited for a weekend to the Roosevelt home at Hyde Park; and during the winter I was regularly invited to parties both by Eleanor Roosevelt and her mother-in-law.

I cannot remember much of what happened at the inaugural ceremony. I seem to remember that when the assemblymen were sworn in Lang took some oath. Franklin D. Roosevelt delivered an eloquent but at the same time colloquial address. He gave the impression that he was talking to a group of friends, which was the impression that he was to give later in his 'fireside talks'. As I listened to him I wondered whether in two years' time he would be taking the oath of office in Washington. It was already apparent that the Republican administration was doomed. But would Roosevelt get the Democratic nomination? Al Smith was waiting in the wings.

I can remember little of the buffet barbecue. The food was, I am sure, admirable, but I can never enjoy a meal that is not accompanied by wine or beer, or preceded by something that is laced with something. My cousin, Claud Cockburn, then the London *Times* man in New York, was there and he and I and Lang went back by train: a slow train that stopped many times. That night Lang took me to see *Late Star Final*, which had opened three days before. The press after the first night left no doubt that it was going to be a considerable success, but the house on this occasion was three-quarters empty. New York was sleeping it off. Two rows in front of me, a woman, in full evening dress, slept uninterruptedly. She did not move even in the intervals. On her shoulder she wore a bedraggled orchid, plunder of the previous night.

I had come over to New York at the end of November. I had long wanted to spend four or five months there, living as I would in London: in a flat of my own, working in the mornings, playing squash racquets, seeing friends, going to films and theatres, absorbing the atmosphere of the city, living as New Yorkers did. It is the only time I have ever rented an apartment in New York. Since then I have stayed at the Algonquin; New York is adapted to hotel life. But these four months at 136 E 36 made me feel that I was a part of New York as I could not have done had I started in an hotel.

One of my first friends in New York was the novelist I. A. R. Wylie. When I told her that I had taken an apartment she advised me to make a picnic life of it. In London I had maintained what amounted to an establishment, with 'the woman who did for me' arriving in time to prepare my breakfast. But in New York – at that time – a maid coming all the way from Harlem charged fifty cents an hour; it was much simpler for a moderately incomed bachelor to go out to breakfast.

It was a bitter winter. Every letter that I received from London spoke of frost and fog; of colds and influenza and broken water-pipes. But in New York, though the puddles in the streets were frozen, though the grass blades in the park were rimmed with frost, five days in seven the sun shone out of a blue sky. I had the feeling of waking to a summer day, in a steam heated room with the sunlight pouring across its floor. It was in a picnic spirit that, with my bath taken, my morning exercises done, I walked to the drug store at the corner of Thirty-fourth and Lexington and, perched on a stool, consumed a twenty-five cent special of orange juice, coffee and hot buttered toast. In London the idea of going out to breakfast at an A.B.C. would have appalled me, but I enjoyed the atmosphere of this busy bar, with its white-coated attendants, wise-cracking with the girls who hastily wolfed their muffins on their way to work, who wore all of them, in spite of the hardness of their lives, a look of smartness, and of gay confidence and defiance; who made a gesture, as they pulled their rabbit fur cloaks round them, and with a toss of their shoulders and a daub of kiss-proof on their pretty mouths went out into the cold. Only young people went there in the mornings. It was later in the day that you found melancholy people drinking bromoseltzers. There was reality there and hopefulness. And it was an hour during which one had need of hopefulness and youth.

My maid Mary did not arrive till half past nine. She was from St Kitts and a Britisher, she proudly told me; her laugh was a genuine West Indian cackle. She screamed with delight when I asked her what her husband did. At first I thought she was telling me that he was a coal heaver, but it was not that. 'He's under de cold earth,' she said. 'Hab you got a job for him?' With her I had none of the leisurely discussions about meals with which time passed so pleasantly in my London flat. Every quarter of an hour of her conversation cost me twelve cents fifty. I encouraged her to make the bed, scour the apartment and prepare a salad for my lunch with all the despatch of which her aged limbs were capable. I used to write till half past eleven, then I would go to a racquet club four blocks away, play for half an hour with the pro, come back to lunch and work through the afternoon. Entertainment of some kind was waiting for me in the evening. I cannot remember spending an evening in my flat alone. Once or twice a week there would be one of those prohibition teas, at which everything would be drunk but tea. Usually those teas ended with my 'going on somewhere else'. Most weeks I made my own modest contribution to the city's gaiety. I would invite ten or twelve friends round for drinks at half past five — we kept earlier hours in those days — arranging that four or five of them would stay on for dinner at some speakeasy. Cocktail parties were, for someone like myself, an easy form of entertainment; there were no elaborate canapés. Janet Post used to serve crisp bacon wrapped round hot toast soaked in peanut butter, but that was beyond my scope. Crackers spread with cream cheese sufficed. I bought gin and whiskey from the pro at the squash racquets club. The whiskey – more often rye than bourbon – was reasonably good, but I did not like the taste of the gin that may or may not have been concocted in a bath-tub. I was not then an *aficionado* of the Five to One Dry Martini – and indeed it took many years for an English barman to learn how to make a Martini that a New Yorker could sip without distaste. I never liked Janet's cocktails, lethally potent though they were. I used to conceal the taste of gin with tinned grapefruit juice, in the proportions of three to one – a kind of gimlet. I thought the mixture excellent but my friends, I was to learn later, were not enthusiastic. When I returned to England I used to serve my gimlets explaining that they were the mode in Manhattan. My friends were delighted with them, but Janet was horrified when, some years later as a weekend guest, she was presented with one of 'Alec's specials'. 'This is too much,' she expostulated. 'It was hard to get French Vermouth in New York during prohibition so we made allowances, but here, no really, there is no excuse.' I learnt then that my friends used to chuckle together over an Englishman's idea of what a cocktail was. It was very polite of them not to have told me at the time.

I also committed the solecism of on occasions filling my hipflask with gin. In California where whiskey was hard to get, gin had been the staple alcoholic commodity. In England where – owing to taxation – there is very little difference in price between the cost of gin and Scotch a host would not be considered parsimonious if he offered a friend a gin and ginger ale. But in New York, where it was cheap, gin occupied the same social status that it had in England in Hogarth's day. A gentleman did not offer a lady gin, but my friends were very patient. I should learn in time; at any rate I was well-intentioned.

I drank too much. Everybody drank too much during prohibition. But I felt remarkably well. New York air then had a tonic, a champagne quality. I could do twice as much there as I could in London, and I could manage on very little sleep. When I drove back at one or two o'clock, my heart would lift at the sight across the park of the incredible skyline of 59th street. How good life was. What a world to be a young man in. I would buy a copy of the *Daily Mirror*, read the 'latest dirt' in Winchell's column, until my eyelids closed. I would shake myself, switch off the light. 'In four hours I'll be ready for anything,' I'd think.

I was working at this time on a novel that was published in England with the title *No Quarter* and in the U.S.A. as *Tropic Seed*. It was a history of piracy told in the form of fiction. It opened in the 1630s with the illegitimate son of a French nobleman running away to sea and joining up with the Buccaneers in Tortuga. It told through a series of separate stories how the strain of piracy ran through the buccaneer's descendants until in the 1930s a business man in Marseilles is proposing to his fellow directors that by issuing a fraudulent company prospectus he and they can raise a million francs on a half million issue, the public being sold the same shares twice.

The novel ended with the following paragraph. 'Doublon rose to his feet. He was such a conventional looking city man in his morning coat, stiff white collar, neatly arranged tie, as you would see in the offices of any big business house in London, New York, Chicago, Paris. It was hard to recognise at a first glance any kinship between this man and the bearded cut-throats who two and a half centuries back had plundered Maracaibo and burnt Panama. But the same blood ran through his veins. That old spirit of the Buccaneers who neither asked quarter nor gave it; whose motto was 'no prey, no pay,' who went ruthlessly for the thing they wanted, who had no use for what was smug and easy, was flaming through Doublon's mind. The same spirit was blazing behind his eyes: the same reckless need of adventure for adventure's sake. His eyes flashed with the old light. Into his voice came the old ruthless ring as he brought down his fist with a crash upon the table. "A gamble?" he said, "yes, a gamble. But gentlemen, what's life for if not to gamble with?"'

The book would at the same time be a history of the West Indies.

I had for some time been wanting to write a history of Haïti and it seemed to me that I could here combine two techniques. I had got the idea eighteen months before, during a trip that I had made down the East African coast, and John Farrar (with whom I had discussed it when I arrived in New York for the launching of *Hot Countries*) thought it would be a good 'follow-up'. A contract was prepared and signed. It was an entirely new kind of venture for me. Up till then my novels had been pictures of contemporary London. In my more roseate moments I pictured reviews that would begin 'Mr Alec Waugh has added a dimension to himself'; but it did not work out that way. John Farrar, when I delivered the manuscript before my return to England, looked dubious. 'I'm not sure that this is quite the book we'd expected.'

'But you want to publish it?'

'Of course, of course.'

Cassell's were not enthusiastic. It was the first novel that I had brought them, and they did not feel that it was the kind of book for which they could launch, as they had hoped, the big publicity campaign that would build me up. Its sales were to be smaller than those of any of my novels since my second and third, which had done very little. It was not the kind of book that library readers had come to expect from me. In America, where I was primarily known as the author of *Hot Countries*, it did rather better, because it was the kind of thing my public did expect, and it had some encouraging reviews. But it was very far from being the success that John Farrar and I had hoped.

I once said to the cutter at my tailors, referring to the suit that I was wearing, 'This suit never turned out quite right.'

'I know, sir, that's what happens to one suit in four.'

The same thing happens to a novel. I know now what was wrong with *No Quarter*. It had no continuous thread of interest. It began with one character, then shifted to another, then a third, a fourth and then a fifth; the theme of piracy was not a sufficiently strong thread to hold the reader's interest. There was no real link between the buccaneers of Tortuga and the planters of colonial France. Maugham, so he tells us in *The Summing Up*, made a similar mistake in his novel *The Merry-Go-Round*. He had felt that life was falsified by taking two or three people, or a group of people, and 'describing their adventures as though no one else existed and nothing else was happening in the world.' He himself was living in several sets that had no connection with one another and he felt that he might give a truer picture of life by carrying on at the same time 'the various stories of equal importance that were enacted during a certain period in different circles.' He constructed therefore five independent stories, which were connected through an elderly woman knowing at least one person in each group. The attempt failed because, in his words, the story lacked 'the continuous line that directs the reader's interest; the stories were not after all of equal importance and it was tiresome to divert one's attention from one set of people to another.' He made another mistake; he did not make the old lady the *raisonneur* of the piece. Later he came to realise that he could have solved his problems by telling the tale in the first person, as he was himself to do in his last major book, *The Razor's Edge*. Writers, it cannot be repeated too often, teach themselves how to write by writing.

Indeed I was myself aware at the time where I had gone wrong. When I was revising the final draft, about a third of the way through I pencilled in the margin, to amuse the friend who was typing it, 'this is where this should have ended'. Up to that point I had concentrated on the illegitimate son of the French nobleman. It ended with him established in the world, a grandfather living in a large house on the edge of the town that is now Cap-Haïtien. One evening he breaks away from the formalities of his daughter's house. He cannot be bothered to wear a heavy brocaded jacket and pointed buckled shoes. Twenty-five pages earlier there had been a description of the kind of shoe that he and his mates had worn at Tortuga; like an Indian moccasin, they were made out of oxhide or pigskin. Having skinned the beast they would place the big toe where the knee had been, then bind the top of a sinew round it. The rest was taken a few inches above the heel and tied there till the skin had dried when, having taken the impress of the man's foot, it would keep in shape.

Tortuga – those were the days, he thinks, as, having broken away from his formal house upon the hill, ridden his unsaddled horse to a dockside tavern, frequented by sailors where the rum is good, he sits with his arms bare, and his shirt open at the throat, sipping at his rum, listening to the sailors' talk.

Presently he is joined by his grandson. 'They were worried up there about you. I was sent to look for you.' To the boy of sixteen, the old man is a figure of respect and awe. He feels very proud sitting there beside him, in silence, sipping at a glass of rum. He could not ask his grandfather too many questions about those days which had already become a part of history. 'You must have had a pretty exciting time, grandfather, in those old days.' The old man shrugs. Yes, he supposed he had, his mind abroad upon his past. Exciting, well, he supposed it had been. But he had an idea that life in the end amounted to much the same. You had too much of a thing or too little of it. You were either on the equator with the sweat running down your face and the fo'castle too hot to sleep in or you were soaked by Antarctic seas, shivering with cold, with your food sodden and sleep only possible in uncertain snatches. For days on end you would be cruising in the Caribbean tacking to desultory July winds, bored, weary, listless, then suddenly you'd sight a sail; you'd give chase to it, there'd be the noise of cannon and the clash of steel, the sockets of your arms would ache with fighting, so that you could cry with the pain of it.

For weeks on end, you would not see a woman: the thought of women would run maddeningly, inflamingly through your brain; then there'd be a sacked city, and suddenly half a dozen exquisite creatures would be yours for the taking, but with yourself so full of liquor that you could scarcely deal satisfactorily with one of them. Too much of a thing or too little of a thing. Whatever the framework of your life that was the way things went. 'You must have enjoyed life in those days, grandfather,' the young man was repeating. The Buccaneer shrugged his shoulders. Yes, perhaps he had. He had found life pretty good all through, but perhaps the days in Tortuga had been his best. 'We wore a pretty comfortable kind of shoe,' he said.

Up to that point I had written a continuous piece of narrative, but from then onwards, the interest was shifted to one group and then another; the reader could put the book aside and feel no need to take it up again. He was no longer being told about the characters in whom he had first been invited to take an interest. The book should have stopped there: but there is no market for a story of thirty thousand words. No one would have published it. Many years later, however, I was to organise a collection of the pieces that I had written about the West Indies between 1928 and 1959. It was called *The Sugar Islands* in England and *Love and the Caribbean* in the U.S.A. In this book I included the first fifty pages of *No Quarter* as a single piece called *The Buccaneer*. It fitted harmoniously into the volume.

III

In the January or February of 1931, the New York telephone company altered the numbering of its subscribers. A numeral took the place of the third letter. Pla-3102 became Pl-9 3102. John O'Hara called his second novel *Butterfield 8* and on its title page, he printed the public announcement of this change. I presume that he did this to date the novel, rather than give it a locale as he did later with *Frederick North Ten*.

The action of *Butterfield 8* was contemporaneous with my own first long visit to New York. My life was, however, very different from that of the majority of the characters in O'Hara's novel; in the first place because I did not have nearly as much money, and secondly, I was not a person who had a fixed place in the New York scene; I was someone who was working his way into it.

When I came to New York in May 1930 for the launching of *Hot Countries*, I knew no New Yorkers except my publisher John Farrar, my agent Carl Brandt, my cousin Claud Cockburn, and two trusted and loved London friends, Hugh Miller, the actor, and his wife, the poetess Olga Katzin. During those three weeks I met a number of people with whom I felt myself on the brink of friendship, in particular Elinor Sherwin, a very pretty socialite in her middle twenties, whom I met at the Millers, and through whom I was later to meet the Langdon Posts. Janet Post, the daughter of Rollin Kirby, the cartoonist, who added to her income as a fashion model, was to become one of my very dearest friends.

I had taken my first steps to becoming a New Yorker, but I was in fact starting very much from scratch when I arrived in New York for the second time, for that four months' visit. I had my own way to make in a strange and foreign city. It was a very big adventure. The average Englishman of my generation who was brought up in the Galsworthian pattern had by the time he was twenty-five met most of the people that he wanted to; at his 'prep', his public school, his university; when, in the early twenties, he embarked on his profession he knew the men with whom he would be working, his colleagues and his rivals. It has been said that in England every one knows every one. And that was true of the Galsworthian world fifty years ago. We had heard of those of our contemporaries whom we had not met, so that when we did meet them we could establish quickly our identities. This added to the intimacy of English life, and because England is a small country geographically, we did not need to make any particular effort to keep up with our old friends. We knew that we should be running into them sooner or later, at this wedding, this cricket match, this race meeting, this or the other anniversary dinner. When on such occasions we met somebody once close to us, we would have a long and cosy chat. We would agree that it was disgraceful that we saw so little of one another. 'We must do something about it,' we would say. But we never would. We would rely on the next meeting, which would surely take place if not this year then the next, and if not then, well then within four years.

This readiness to rely on chance encounters is one of the many themes that thread their way through Anthony Powell's *The Music of Time*. It also adds to the fascination of London's social life. It makes every occasion an adventure; you never know which old friends you may not meet at lunch or cocktails.

This explains why the English do not show much enthusiasm when friends from abroad turn up in England. Many Americans and many Britons who are stationed abroad feel resentful after having entertained Britons lavishly in their own countries, at rating only a dish of tea when they turn up in England. Henry James has written about this in *International Episode* and so has Noël Coward in *Hands Across the Sea*. Yet how often have I, delighted though I am to welcome a friend in Tangier or New York, felt my heart sink when a quite dear couple announce their intention of turning up in London. I have looked at my diary in dismay. 'How on earth am I going to fit them in?' It is not that I am doing anything of any real concern; it is just that I do not seem to have an evening free until the week after next. It is all a part of our English pattern of keeping in touch with our old friends; of

17

keeping in touch with ourselves I might almost say, for our friends are ourselves: they are a part of our lives.

This is a fact that one realises more and more acutely as one reaches one's later sixties; one sees a friend's name in the obituary column, and one thinks 'Now I'll never be able to talk about any of that again.'

There is a great deal to be said for the insularly exclusive manner in which Edwardian and early Georgian Londoners organised their social life, but there is every bit as much to be said for the informal manner in which New Yorkers organised their lives forty years ago. There was, too, this primary difference that New York is a port; that men come there to make a living. It has been said that no one is born in New York and that no one dies there. Hospital and cemetery statistics disprove this. But there is admittedly an atmosphere of transience, a coming and going. London is a port, too, but few Londoners are aware of that. In New York, in the twenties and the thirties, you were always conscious of the liners that you saw from your office and apartment windows. There was a feeling, in consequence, that you had very little time, that you had to make the most of every contact quickly. I was told as a young bachelor in London that if you met at a party a young woman whom you found attractive, it was good manners to ask the hostess if she could arrange a second meeting. In New York if you did not ring up such a person the first thing next morning, it was likely to be the last you saw of her.

In 1931 informality was increased by prohibition. In quite a number of homes, alcohol was not served. In hotels you had to rely upon a hip flask. A great many people preferred speakeasies. I hardly ever went into a club. I now spend a great deal of my time in New York in the Century on 7 W 43rd and in the Coffee House which is two blocks over on 45th. During prohibition, I was twice taken to the Coffee House by Charles Hanson Towne. I was not offered a cocktail or a highball. In his own apartment Towne was a punctilious host. I have no idea whether or not it was possible to obtain an alcoholic drink at the Coffee House during prohibition. I have asked a number of the older members but none of them can remember what the arrangements were. Once

Stanley Rinehart took me to the Harvard Club with Bob Winans, Katherine Brush's husband, where we heightened our enjoyment of an admirable steak with a flask of authentic Bourbon. I remember drinking a highball in the locker room. Did we take the flask into the dining-room, or was the steak served in the locker room?

Carl Brandt gave me a card to the Players' Club. There are few pleasanter club houses. I dined there once, to see what it was like. I remember thinking 'this place would be heaven without prohibition', as indeed it is today. But I had no wish to go again. I could not imagine myself enjoying masculine society without the stimulus of alcohol. I am sure that members of clubs had their private stores of alcohol on the premises. But where they did their drinking I have no idea. I wish, for the purposes of history, that I had given myself that particular research assignment, but in a city so companionably supplied with attractive and not unpermissive females, I felt I could leave club life until my return to London.

Within a very short time my days were crowded. Every party that I went to was an adventure; I was bound to meet someone new who would throw a new light upon the life of this exciting city. The depression was growing more intense every week. Hoover had talked of 'prosperity being round the corner'. But no one believed him any longer. The thing had to run its course. To say that one had a good time during the depression, will not, I hope, sound an equivalent of a Frenchman's having had a good time in Paris during the Occupation, but if one is thirty-two years old, in good health with one's circumstances promising, one is likely to be having a good time anyhow. There was a lot of talk about the depression but it was a dramatic gloominess. Elinor said, 'When all the men were telling you how much money they had made that day, you could act bored and say "let's talk of something else". You have to try and be sympathetic when they tell you how much they've lost.'

Many people did lose a lot of money. But was it real money? Was it capital on the interest of which a way of life was built? I have heard men and women now in their fifties talk of being

19

'children of the depression'. What exactly does that mean? A holiday to Europe cancelled; a move into a smaller flat; a mortgage closed; payments not kept up on a car or house? I have heard stories of the unemployed riding on freight cars across the country. There were queues for the soup kitchens in Times Square. There were the apples for the unemployed on sale at five cents a piece. Janet Post used to put them on her cocktail tray with canapés stuck into them on toothpicks. One of her friends said 'Should you be doing that? Aren't they for the unemployed?' But then there were the unemployed in England. There was the march of the Welsh miners. Usually someone was having a bad time somewhere and the social conscience had not yet got adjusted to a feeling that everyone was entitled to a good time: that poverty was not a misfortune but a crime committed by the state. But mainly, primarily, the distinctive feature about the depression in New York in January 1931 was that it was not depressing. It was dramatic, to be discussed eagerly, with voices raised if need be.

It was hard to tell how serious was its effect upon the book trade. In the previous summer Farrar and Rinehart and one or two other publishers had made the experiment of issuing new novels in hard covers at a dollar. The experiment did not work and was soon abandoned. But did it involve Farrar and Rinehart in a heavy loss? 'One thing breaks even with another,' was John's view of it. Was it a case of Chinese profit – the Chinese merchant who complains that he has had a wretched year; that he has lost a million dollars. He had expected his trading to show a profit of seven million dollars. He has only shown one of six.

The theatre in New York – as happens so often in difficult times – was doing well, and there were some fine plays on the boards. *Green Pastures, Once in a Lifetime, Grand Hotel, Private Lives, The Greeks had a Word for It, Tomorrow and Tomorrow, Lysistrata, On the Spot.* Magazines were not paying the high prices that they had three years before, and editors were tending to use the stories that they had in their inventories. But there were a great many magazines on the market. A reasonable story found a purchaser. Most of the writers I was meeting were managing well enough. But the great thing about it all was the dramatic tension that New York always manages to produce. Whenever I go there, I feel that I am having my batteries recharged. People are interested in what their friends are doing. You become interested in your own work again. It is probably because of our climate, that we English wear a defensive armour of apathy. You lay elaborate plans for a garden party, for a cricket match, a picnic. At the moment of writing this section I am laying plans so that I shall watch the Test Match at Lord's in June 1975, but it is pointless of me to get excited over it: as likely as not the match will be spoilt by rain as were the matches against Australia in 1964, and 1968. The English have to be phlegmatic. In New York where the climate swings from one extreme to another, only a mercurial temperament can stand the strain. You have to let yourself swing. That was the thing about the depression in New York. It was not depressing.

Prohibition added to the dramatic atmosphere of the day's routine. Every drink was an adventure; every drink was a protest against an outrageous imposition of authority. There was a growing feeling too that authority was beginning to doubt the wisdom of the Volstead Act. When the stock market was booming, it was not illogical to attribute prosperity to prohibition. There were no black Mondays nowadays. A man did a full week's work, and anyhow prohibition was better than no drink at all. But now there was not enough work to keep a man occupied for half a week; gangsters were in control of civic management; bootleggers were running the country; the young were ruining their health. Protests grew stronger. Voices of hope were raised.

The New Yorker's 'Talk of the Town' reported that 'a cordial letter, lying open on our desk from Berry Bros. & Co. of 3 St James's Street, London, has been responsible for the low fever we've been running all week. The letter says that Berry Bros. have noticed that changes were taking place in the Prohibition law over here and that they hope in a few years wines will be restored to American cellars. With that in mind they wonder if we wouldn't like to buy some wines and whiskys to be kept in England until they could be legally imported. Rarely has our spirit been swept upward higher in the realms of pure fancy. In

21

fact we were so carried away that we began making all sorts of plans, including the presentation of a bottle of synthetic gin to the museum of the City of New York.'

Each highball was not only a gesture of defiance, but a symbol of imminent victory. With the economy in the condition that it was, the country could not afford prohibition, and episodes like the St Valentine's Day Massacre were getting the country a bad name. A great deal of one's talk turned on alcohol. One after another the guests at an evening party would embark on a saga of their previous evening's drinking. 'First of all, we went to that Italian place on W 48. You know the one, between 7th and 8th. We had a couple of daiquiris, but Jack said they were too sweet, so we went a block across to Tony's and they certainly were drier there. So we had a couple then Maggie said she was feeling hungry, but Frank said No, they must try Mario's first.'

On and on it went and the audience would be genuinely interested, interjecting appropriate comments and enquiries; then when one saga was rounded off, the next member of the party would start in with 'Well, I'll tell you what happened to me. . . .' After the last traveller had told his story, the comparison of hangovers would begin. Was it best to take a prairie oyster before you went to sleep or start right in next morning with a pick-me-up? Everyone drank a great deal too much and much of it was deleterious stuff. During my last days Elinor said to me, 'I'm glad that you are leaving next week.' It was a shock. I had hoped that she would miss me. 'If you stayed on here, drinking all this bootleg gin, you'd have a stomach ulcer by September,' and indeed not so many of the men I drank with then are still around, and those that are, are, for the most part, alcoholics anonymous.

A large proportion of *The New Yorker* magazine jokes turned on alcohol. *The New Yorker* was in its sixth year. It was the new thing and its vitality and originality added considerably to the gaiety of New York life. How eagerly I went out each Friday morning to the bookstalls. It was presenting to the public a whole group of new writers and artists who were making a more powerful impact as a team than they had as individuals – Ogden Nash, Thurber, Wolcott Gibbs, John O'Hara, Peter Arno, Soglow,

22

Helen Hokinson. There was a family atmosphere about the magazine. Dorothy Parker was sitting in on the drama page for Robert Benchley who was in Hollywood. At the end of her column she would include in italics, *Personal Robert Benchley. Please come home. Nothing is forgiven*, or, *R.B. Please come home. A joke's a joke*. When *The New Yorker* was making such blithe fun of the current scene, it was impossible to take the depression too seriously. Garrett Price's picture of the city tycoon saying to a meek petitioner 'When you are asking for a raise now, you are attacking American business. You wouldn't attack American business, would you, Smith?' contrasted with Helen Hokinson's clubwoman's squeak, 'A baby right here on Park Avenue. What an amazing city.'

Wolcott Gibbs in an obituary paragraph on Helen Morgan, which he printed later in *Season in the Sun*, said how her death brought back 'all the dark illicit little rooms we used to sit in full of love for our fellow law-breakers, full of large theories about nothing, full of juniper berries and glycerine.' He would, he said, be 'missing her songs, just as we have long missed all the other things that went with them, the chained and mysterious door, the proprietor reputed to be a celebrated gunman.'

There was a genuine romance about those speakeasies. But oddly enough the speakeasy of which I have the warmest memories is one that had no ritual of chains and protective gunmen. It stood wide open to the street. It was called then, as it is called today, the Passy, and its appearance has not changed; though in those days it had no canopy. You walked straight in, without being questioned. It served good cocktails, good wine and a variety of liqueurs. When Michael Arlen visited New York in 1931, it was there that I invited him to meet Elinor Sherwin, and Selma Robinson, then publicity greyhound for the Literary Guild, who is still (I am glad to say) very much around. I never knew how the place was protected. When I returned in 1936 it was to find the same brisk head waiter there.

In the middle of January I began a lecture tour under the auspices of W. Colston Leigh. The belief was generally held, in England in the '20s, that there was a great deal of money to be made on the lecture platform in the U.S.A. There may have been in the early '20s, but by the end of the decade English lecturers had ruined the market by their casualness and patronising manners. Certainly there was not much left in 1931; at any rate for me. I was at Leigh's behest for ten weeks. He paid me an advance of $1,000. He took half of the fee that he received from the society to which I lectured. He paid my travel expenses, first class. But not my hotel bills. He arranged seven or eight lectures for me. I went as far west as Grand Rapids and as far north as Portland, Maine. The highest fee I received was $200 from the English Club in Rhode Island; the lowest $50 from a public library in Kansas. It would not have paid Leigh to send me there for $25 but I was lecturing at Grand Rapids the next day. My fees did not earn the advance of $1,000. But I suppose that Leigh just broke even on the deal.

It would not have paid me to cross the Atlantic and spend ten weeks in the country for $1,000. It only paid me because I wanted to see more of the country. In 1960 and 1963 I undertook two quite ambitious tours for Colston Leigh. I was then, as the author of *Island in the Sun*, very much better known than I had been in 1930. They were coast to coast tours, lasting three months, with thirty-five engagements each. The fees were higher by then, with $500 at the Library of Congress as the highest. The terms were the same, the agency paying for my transport, and taking half the fees. My share of the profits worked out at some $4,500. But my hotel expenses cut that figure down by half. I paid tax on a sum of $2,500 – not a very large return for three months' work, as the lectures needed preparing in advance. Moreover, a tour leaves one exhausted, in need of a holiday. A lecture tour is really only worthwhile if you like lecturing, which as a matter of fact I do.

A lecture tour is, moreover, a break in one's routine. It is an equivalent for the practice of rotating crops. One comes fresher to writing after a few weeks on the platform. Moreover, there are certain indirect emoluments. One enlarges one's public. One gets publicity for one's books. My 1960 tour coincided with the publication of my novel *Fuel for the Flame* and my 1963 tour with that of my first autobiography. Some members of my audiences must have bought my books or at least asked for them at their local library. But it is very easy to over-rate the extent of such returns. There were one or two writers who specialised on the lecture field. John Mason Brown was one, and between the wars the Englishman S. K. Ratcliffe. But for the average reasonably established writer, lecturing is one of several irons in the fire. It really boils down to this. 'Do you or don't you get a kick out of it?' I did.

An average lecture engagement would run like this: you would have spent the night in the train. A great many people do not like trains. I happen to, and sleep well on them. You arrive at the city where you are to lecture round about ten o'clock. You are met at the station by the secretary. She is far from resembling a Helen Hokinson caricature of the Club Woman. She is usually an elegant, well produced, personable matron in her middle forties or fifties. She will outline your morning's programme. Your talk is to start at two o'clock. At twelve thirty there will be a lunch at the Country Club. After the talk there will be a tea. Your train leaves at nine forty-five. One of the committee has suggested that you would like to have dinner with her family. It will give you an opportunity to see an American home. In the meantime she would suggest a drive round the town; after which perhaps you would like to read over your notes.

It is a strenuous programme, and your actual lecture is the least exhausting feature of it. You are on parade, and all the time you are fulfilling an ambassadorial function, since quite a few people are going to judge your country by your behaviour. The English had not got themselves a good reputation in the U.S.A. during the 1920s – not only on the lecture platform but as self-appointed guests. They had abused the hospitality they had invited, by running up bills, borrowing cars and charging up the petrol. Perhaps in some cases Americans had brought this treatment on themselves by boasting about 'the almighty dollar'; but a great many minor English socialites overplayed their hands on the strength of an accent and well-cut clothes. In 1927 they had jokes in Pebble beach – 'How many bills did the Leytons leave behind? Is that all, you were lucky. The Fergusons took us for a genuine ride.' They could afford to laugh about it when the stock market was booming. It was less funny now. In the club car of the first train in which I crossed America, I read in *Harper's Bazaar* a story by Charles Hanson Towne called *Much Adieu about Nothing* in which a supercilious and patronising British novelist was taught a lesson. It certainly taught me one. I resolved that I would do my best to counteract that impression.

My role as a lecturer was not made any the easier by prohibition. I was not, at the age of thirty-two, as dependent upon alcohol as I am today, but even then I should have found the lunch parties that preceded my talks very much easier if they had been accompanied by a glass or two of wine. I never travelled without a hip flask but I was chary of resorting to it during the half hour when I was 'going over my notes'. Vodka was not available in those days and I did not want to breathe synthetic gin over the committee.

I was conscious that my lectures in 1960 and 1963 went a great deal better than had those that I delivered in 1931. I do not know if the lectures were any better. They may have been. But the presence of wine at meals and cocktails at receptions made, as I had suspected that they would, a considerable difference to the general atmosphere. There was another difference, which in 1931 I had not anticipated. In 1931 when I was thirty-two years old I was facing an audience most of whose members were quite a little older than myself. In 1960, when I was sixty-two, I was addressing women between the ages of forty and fifty-five, the ages which I found then particularly seductive. I felt myself to be facing an herbaceous border, privileged to be in the presence of such attractive females. I exerted myself to entertain them. They recognised that I was stimulated by them. There was in consequence on their side an instantaneous response. I got a definite kick out of my lectures.

As I have already told, I had brought out with me from London the manuscript of a book of short stories, entitled *Most Women*. Illustrated by Lynd Ward it was to be a companion volume to *Hot Countries*. In the course of my New York chapter, I sketched my own routine there.

'There are very few interruptions to my day,' I wrote. 'New York may contain as many idle people as London does. But I have not met them. Nobody rings me up to tell me about a headache. Such necessary interruptions as may come can be dealt with easily. I have usually got through two thousand words before the Chanin Building has begun to hang high over Lexington its patches of oblong light. . . . No doubt for the person for whom New York is a home, the manipulation of acquaintances and friends is as complicated a business as it is in London; with engagement diaries black with dates a fortnight off. But possibly because of a certain improvised quality in New York life, but in a greater degree, I think, because of the American's great readiness to hospitality, the foreigner with a few real friends and a number of acquaintances does not need to plan his amusements far ahead. I know that I who have never found it possible to get any solid work done in London, should never have believed it possible that in a big city one could get through so much work at a time when one was having so much fun. Nor that leading a town life one could feel so astonishingly well.'

I wrote that in mid-December. It had ceased to be true by mid-January when I started lecturing. My acquaintance had quadrupled. Each party had led to another party. The two parties became four parties, and the four eight. Carl Brandt was then strenuously courting a rival agent Carol Hill to whom he was to be married the following summer. One friend became two friends. I had barely met during the summer Stanley Rinehart's brother Alan. He had ceased to occupy an office in the family firm. He was at work upon a play. He had a wife as wealthy as she was beautiful whose father had once held post at the Court of St James. He was to become a real *copain* of mine. Claud Cockburn was currently courting Francis Hope Hale who, a year later, was to become his wife. My diary grew blacker. I became a courtier of Mrs Delano Roosevelt. I took her to see *Private Lives*. Her voice deepened when she said of Noël Coward and Gertrude Lawrence, 'I think they must be in love, don't you?' Charles Hanson Towne gave a lunch party where I met three of his favourite hostesses. One of them, Mollie Potter, became one of mine. Langdon Post was often away on political assignments, leaving Janet at a loose end in the evenings. I met her father, Rollin Kirby. There was a constant going and coming in her apartment. I had brought out with me from England letters of introduction to Carl van Vechten and Edward Wasserman (later Waterman). One of Farrar and Rinehart's most important authors was Katherine Brush, whose *Young Man of Manhattan* had been one of the best sellers of the previous year. The Farrars and the Rineharts were often giving 'teas' for their new books. A number of Englishmen paid brief visits including Michael Arlen and Henry Williamson. Then there was Emma Mills, who was to become a very good friend of mine. She *was* a Helen Hokinson caricature, of medium height, thin, ageless, with encasing garments and hats that were, I am sure, expensive but looked as though they had been acquired at a jumble sale. She organised a series of Book and Authors mornings and lunches at the Biltmore, which were attended by a loyal group of affluent upper-crust women. The lunches would be attended by a number of prominent writers, six or seven of whom Miss Mills would introduce by name, and two or three of whom would make short speeches. The mornings lasted for an hour. Coffee and bouillon were served. Miss Mills would talk about contemporary books and she would introduce to her audience a couple of well known writers who would speak for ten to five minutes each. She was not an eloquent speaker herself, she was not humorous, but she deeply cared for books and writers, and her audience had confidence in her. They followed her advice. I cannot think how she ever got started. No lecture agent could have thought 'This is the woman for my list.' She was an ardent anglophil. Every summer she came over to England. She learnt what was in the air. She found out which writers were coming to New York in the winter. They promised her that they would speak at one of her lunches or her mornings. She had a number of quite rich friends, one of whom would give a lunch party after the morning session. These were lively occasions. That was how I met André Maurois, Oliver La Farge and Stephen Vincent Benet. Another of her friends had a box at the Metropolitan. It would have been easy to make fun of Emma Mills, and several people did, but she was a warm, dear person. She did a lot for writers, and she was on the right side: by that I mean that when an 'avant-garde' book or play was being discussed, she would warn her audience. 'I am not sure that all of you will like this book, but I do believe that in thirty years' time, young people will be saying to you "Now how did you feel about *Joseph in Jeopardy* when it first came out?"' I became very fond of her, and my friendship with her considerably added to the entries in my diary. In addition to all of this, I found myself involved in a love affair of which I have the happiest memories.

I had in fact, become every bit as much a resident of New York as, one year earlier, I had been a resident of London, and here, every bit as much as there, I found it impossible to concentrate upon my work when I was leading an animated metropolitan life.

In the early '20s when I had a half-time job in my father's publishing house, Chapman & Hall, spending Mondays and Fridays in his office, I used during the football season, between mid-September and mid-April, to catch a train every Monday night to a small town in Metroland called Radlett, two miles walk from which was the village of Shenley. In its local inn, The White Horse – my board and lodging cost eight shillings a day – I wrote solidly for three days. On the Friday morning I returned to London; I spent the night with my parents; on the Saturday I played football for Rosslyn Park. During Sunday I was a social Londoner. London in the winter, in those days, was a lively and animated city.

This pattern had proved very satisfactory, and I realised that if I was to get my novel finished before I sailed for England I should have to find some equivalent for The White Horse at Shenley. It was not too easy. There is no equivalent in the U.S.A. for the English village 'pub' within easy reach of London which has a couple of bedrooms available for the casual motorist. Indeed, when American troops were in England during the Second War they found the village pub one of the most endearing as unusual features of English life. In 1931 the motel did not exist. In the end I found a comfortable hotel two miles from New London, where I

29

put in three solid weeks of writing and had my novel finished by the second week in March.

I was due to sail on March 24th. I was taking the 'Lafayette' – one of the French Line's newest but slower ships. It sailed at 11.30 a.m., so there could be no 'pouring' on to her on the night before. I arranged to have a supper in my flat, then we could go down to the village, to the county fair. There were about twelve guests. Elinor Sherwin was there, the Langdon Posts, Carl Brandt – Carol was in London; I fancy that it was during that visit to London that they decided that they might as well get married – Claud Cockburn, probably Hope Hale, Henry Williamson, John Farrar and his wife, Alan Rinehart was away, but Stanley was there. And of course the girl whose omnipresence after January had decided me that if I was to get my novel finished, I must leave New York.

They were the dozen out of the thirty people that I had been seeing most of in New York, of whom I had grown the fondest. Of the last eleven months I had spent five in New York, which was a greater time than I had spent in any city during the last six years. I had become identified with the city's life, and these dozen people were the core of my life there. It was strange to realise that in eighteen hours I would have cut the threads that bound me to their lives. I had no idea when I would be coming back. I'll be coming back soon, I said, and of course I should some day. New York was a base, an essential base for a writer. But should I ever be here for so long a time again?

As I waited for the first guests to arrive, I reflected that several of them had not known each other a year ago; that though they were now good friends they had only become friends because I had been their catalyst. When I had gone, would half of them ever see each other again? They would return to the pattern of their own lives; when they met in the street or in a bar they would say 'Have you heard anything of Alec lately? Have you any idea when he will be coming over?'

I had no idea then that New York would become a second, if not a first, home for me so that I should become in my small way a centre of a group – so that people would be saying 'we never seem to see each other except when Alec's here.'

I am always happier as a host than as a guest. I enjoy bringing friends into a life of my own: which is something that you can do in a city the size of New York, and which you have to be on your guard against in small communities like a West Indian island. I have several times heard West Indians complain that visitors arrive with letters of introduction to members of different groups. They are entertained by those groups, then they start entertaining back people who know about one another, quite like one another, but don't want to meet each other at intimate dinner parties. Even in London you have to be careful. When I married, several old friends complained to my wife that 'they never knew whom they would meet at Alec's.' I would have thought that was a compliment to my versatility as a man about town. But it was not intended that way. In New York that would not be true. New Yorkers are always ready to welcome the newcomer.

Of the friends that I made during those four and half months, only four are still active in the city's life – Carol Hill, Selma Robinson, Donita Borden and Benjamin Sonnenberg. Ben was then at the start of his spectacular rise to prominence. One of his many concerns at that time was the publicity of the Hotel Chatham. When I arrived in New York in April 1930 for the fêting of *Hot Countries* it was in a suite there that I was installed. Our paths were to cross frequently during the next few years; then in 1950 when Lipton's needed a book written on Sir Thomas, Ben, who handled Lipton's publicity, thought of me. What a number of receptions at his sumptuous house in Grammercy Park have I not attended since. He is in as lively form as ever. I suppose I should be grateful that as many as four of my 1930 friends are still around. Forty-four years is a long time.

On my last morning Janet Post drove down with me to the docks. I organised my luggage then we pushed our way through the crowded promenade to the upper deck. We found a corner sheltered from the wind. The sun was shining; the tall towers of Manhattan looked very lovely in its amber radiance against the blue expanse of sky. We gossiped casually and easily. We knew that we should meet again. Her sister-in-law was married to an Englishman. She came over to England every other year. Besides, *nôtre tendresse* – there is no word for it in English – had gone very deep. The siren hooted, a bellboy came along the decks beating upon a gong. 'I'd better be on my way,' said Janet.

The Langdon Posts are no longer married, and Janet, now the wife of William Banning, lives in a ranch in Southern California, in Duarte. I have paid many visits there. Only a few months ago at Easter I was bathing in her swimming pool, when New York was recovering from the snow storm that had drenched the bonnets of the Easter Parade. Forty years have not marred her beauty. She is as slim and elegant as ever. The other day in London, at the Athenaeum, I showed a recent photograph of her to one of her Cambridge beaux. 'She looks the same,' he said.

IV

There are quite a few things that I miss in this 'Brave New World' – nothing more than transatlantic crossings. Whenever I can I still make the crossing by sea, but it is becoming increasingly hard to arrange one's travel in terms of the sea. Ships nowadays make their money out of cruises. They provide holidays afloat – not transportation. Moreover, you meet nowadays a different class of traveller by sea. Up till 1939, anyone who wanted to cross from England to New York had to go by sea. You were likely to find on board a minister of state, a prominent actress, a socialite in the news, the heir to a Dukedom. You met on equal terms men and women whom you would not expect to meet in the ordinary routine of your life: and you were quite likely to have a real talk with them. Formal persons were ready to relax on board. Nowadays such people have not the time to go by sea. You are only likely to meet on board elderly and retired people for whom time is of no importance; and families who are moving their residences with not only luggage but furniture and possessions. Thirty-five years ago, during the three or four days before I sailed I would be making enquiries to find out who would be on board. New York friends would be saying, 'What luck for you, you'll meet Frank and Elsie.' The seeing off and the meeting of ships was part of the city's life, part of the city's drama. Newspapers carried 'on the gangplank' columns.

There was animated discussion as to which lines were the most attractive. The French line had the admirable slogan 'You are in France the moment you step aboard.' Personally, I rarely travelled by a British ship because I wanted to be in a foreign atmosphere. I saw enough of my compatriots at home. I usually travelled French, because of my love both of France and the French cuisine. Moreover, they served complimentary table wine which for me reduced the cost of a trip considerably.

I usually travelled by the eight or nine day boats. They were cheaper, they were as comfortable, and – what was important – they gave me the length of time aboard that I needed to write a short story. I can only work when I live in an atmosphere of day to day eventlessness. A man friend of long standing told me that he rarely failed to have a love affair on board. 'I don't know how else one fills in the time.' Though I met Ruth on a liner coming up from Tahiti to San Francisco, I have never had a romance on board, except when I have brought a travelling companion with me.

On the first day out, I settle down to my manuscript directly after breakfast, and by the last day have completed the story that will pay my passage. On westbound trips when the clock goes forward, I would find myself waking later every day and after the second day would start missing lunch.

The trip on the 'Lafayette' was no exception, apart from the fact that I was working on articles not short stories. Whenever possible I try to get a table by myself on board: that leaves me freer to make my own friends. This time it was not possible, but I am glad that it was not, because I found myself at a table alone with a very charming young woman called Sally Edmondson, whose parents ran the Coca-Cola plant in Anniston, Alabama. We had become friends by the time that the ship docked. We kept up with one another and a year later I visited her in Anniston. They arranged a picnic excursion that gave me a new angle on American *mores*. A group of about thirty, youngish men and women, drove out into the country, I should say some seventy miles away. We stayed in a barn beside a river. The men slept in one room, the women in another. We had brought mattresses. We cooked ourselves a stew with hamburgers and hot dogs. After the meal we sat round an open fire, with banjos, sometimes singing, now and again playing guessing games, 'Truths' and things like that. There was no hard liquor. No one brought a hip flask. We drank Coca-Cola. It was all very fresh and healthy; how different from the conventional picture of the average débutante's wild party. On that picnic I met Sally Henderson Hay, the poetess, whom I was to find over twenty years later in the Macdowell Colony at Peterboro' New Hampshire.

In Washington, after the war, I was to re-meet my hostess, by which time her husband was a Colonel stationed in the Pentagon. She was to give me an amusing example of Anglo–American misunderstanding. She had had a mild attack of 'flu in London and had asked the hotel to send a doctor. She had had the right medicine provided and a couple of weeks later had received his bill. It had been marked 'with compliments'. She had taken this to mean that his visit was complimentary. She had thought how very gracious of him 'to treat me free, because I am a lone American in London.' It was not till a long time later that she learnt that it was customary in England to present bills marked 'with compliments': by then she had forgotten not only his name but that of the hotel. She felt very badly about that. 'He'll think Americans don't pay their bills'; I told her that Americans *knew* that a great many of the English never paid their bills.

My friendship with Sally Edmondson was typical of quite a number of such friendships that I was to make in future years. Travelling around, for the most part, even in my married period, as an unattached male, I was frequently making contacts with attractive females whom I met in boats, in trains, and at parties. One of the pleasantest features of our emancipated modern world is the freedom that it gives to men and women to make friendships that have no ulterior objective. I do not suppose that any man knows exactly what is at the back of his mind the first time he asks a woman out to dinner; if he is wise he thinks: 'This is someone I am sure that I could get to like. Let's see how it turns out.' Now and again of course he is on the brink of a romance, but very often he is not, and he is starting one of those friendships which have their own special quality because they are with a woman, and because the spark which starts them is a flicker of mutual physical attraction. Margaret Lane has written a very charming essay on this subject called *Amitié Amoureuse*. Such friendships enrich a man's life, and a woman's too, immeasurably. They have also in my case enlarged considerably my knowledge of the United States. I should never have gone to Anniston, Alabama, but for Sally Edmondson.

A friendship started on the 'Columbus' in June 1930 has made Albuquerque one of my ports of call for forty years. I have not been limited to the towns to which my lecture agent books me or my publisher sends me in the interests of publicity.

There was another enlivening fellow traveller on the 'Lafayette', the *Saturday Evening Post* short story writer Richard Connell: he was one of Carl Brandt's clients and was a few years older than myself. We soon found we had a great deal in common. On the second or third day out he said, 'I've read one or two of your books and liked them, I don't suppose you've read a line of mine.'

'I don't often read the *Saturday Evening Post*,' I said.

'If you did, I don't suppose you'd remember me; that's the worst of writing for magazines. No one's ever heard of you. Which magazines do you read?'

'*The New Yorker* and *Cosmopolitan*.'

'You would. That's not being rude. They both specialise in writers whom you've heard of through their books. No one knows by name anyone who writes only for magazines; immense though the circulation of those magazines may be.'

He did not seem in the least bitter about it. He was simply stating a fact.

'I'd have thought,' I said, 'that magazine readers would have their favourite authors.'

'You'd think so. Editors would like to think so and agents persuade them that they must raise the prices for their favourites. But you can't persuade any magazine writer that they have. I've hardly ever met a reader who has heard of me, and if I do, he thinks that I have written something that I haven't.'

'Haven't you ever published a selection of your stories in a book?'

'Who'd want to pay two dollars fifty for what he can get for a dime: all by the same author too!'

As far as I knew I had never read one of Connell's stories, and I never have. Whenever I turned over a copy of the *Saturday Evening Post* on a bookstall, it was not to find him there. He was a very successful writer in his day.

I was planning to spend only a very short while in England, less than two weeks; I was anxious to reach Villefranche and get down to work on a solid contemporary novel. I needed to get down on paper both my experiences in the U.S.A. and my Californian romance: I had reached, I felt, the point when I could recollect that particular emotion in tranquillity.

With only ten or so days available, I could make no attempt to pick up the threads of my London life. Experience of the past had counselled me how carefully I had to plan my returns in advance, issuing invitations from abroad for this luncheon or that dinner. When I had first begun to travel in June 1926, it had taken me a long time to break my threads with English life. There were so many things I wanted to do next month or the week after that. A few pages back I explained how interwoven was the pattern of English social life. The Londoner who returns to the city of his birth after a seven-month absence without previous preparation is met on the telephone by an unenthusiastic, 'Oh, so you've been away? I thought I hadn't seen you at the Savile lately.'

You suggest that it would be nice if you could get together. There is a tepid agreement, then a pause. 'Couldn't you dine or lunch with me?' you ask. 'That's very nice of you. I'm pretty booked this week, next week too for that matter.'

You arrange a meeting for the Friday fortnight. Three weeks after that just when you are packing to take off again, he calls to ask if you can dine with him in two weeks' time. 'I'm so sorry,' you say, 'I am leaving for New York next Thursday.'

'You are. Too bad. Let me know next time you're back.'

Even so I was excited about my return to England. I was eager to see my parents. London was my base. I had my flat in Chelsea. It was actually in the Royal Hospital Road; it was called Cheyne Place because the proprietor considered that that sounds better as an address and could therefore command a higher rate. It was an unfurnished four-room flat. I also had a secondary base in my parents house, Underhill, 145 North End Road, a quarter of a mile south of Golders Green tube station. My father had built the house in 1907. Evelyn had spent his childhood there and I my boyhood. It was a comfortable three-storeyed house, typical of the suburban houses that were being built round London in the first years of the century. When I married for the first time in 1919 I converted the old nursery into a library sitting-room. I still kept a number of my possessions there, and so did Evelyn; particularly our clothes. We were a united family. Underhill was very much a home.

At the end of 1929 my father retired from the managing directorship of Chapman and Hall, but he remained chairman and literary adviser. At Underhill he turned my old sitting-room into his study.

When he retired he began to keep a daily journal in one of Boots' commercial diaries. Ten lines were available to every day and with his small Greek script he could get twenty-five words in a line. He set high store by these diaries; but though they have a deep interest for me, they could scarcely be of interest to the general public, so full are they of names of whom only the family had heard. I presented his diaries – all except that of his last year – to the Boston University Libraries. Last spring, I asked the library to lend me a copy of the 1931 diary.

During the first months of the year, he was at work upon his autobiography, *One Man's Road*, which was published in the autumn. He was not well that winter. He notes that he did not take his first afternoon walk until February 3rd. His doctor advised him to take things quietly and have breakfast in bed. Yet he was writing two thousand words a day on his book, in addition to reading MSS for Chapman and Hall, writing reports on them and conducting a vigorous correspondence.

Evelyn was abroad, on his first trip to Abyssinia for the King's coronation. Children tend to imagine that their parents' lives revolve round them, and because parents make themselves available at a moment's notice, putting off guests, cancelling acceptances, they picture their parents' lives as ceasing when they themselves go abroad, as in *The Blue Bird* the grandparents vanish when the young people cease to think of them. It was not until I read these diaries that I realised how very occupied my parents were; what a constant coming and going there was. 'Alec came out to lunch to say goodbye before leaving for America. Read a novel by Beatrice Kean Seymour: fairly good. Rosemary came to tea, she told me. . . . While she was still there Aubrey rang up to ask if he could call after dinner.' One person after another, and that was how it went on, right to the last week of his life in late June, 1943. He died early in the morning of Saturday 26th. He had tried to write his diary on the Wednesday but his script was illegible. He dictated the Thursday's entry to my mother, but on the previous Saturday he had been watching cricket all day at the Highgate school ground.

Evelyn was back from Abyssinia on March 9th. My father's diary announced that he looked 'very hearty and rosy and well', bringing many delightful gifts – carved animals and a canvas picture of the Abyssinian farmer's life. My father describes Evelyn as spending many hours opening letters. He had probably received no mail for several months. Two days later he lunches with Duckworth's partner Tom Balston and pockets a cheque for £260 on royalties from *Labels*; at the next board meeting Chapman and Hall signed for him a cheque for £117 which does not seem a large amount in view of the fact that *Vile Bodies* had been published in the spring of 1930 and he had not received a large advance. He took his mother to the Ritz for tea. She enjoyed its splendour. He went to see the Plunkett Greens at Littlehampton, thence to Brighton where Harry Preston feasted him at the Albany with oysters and champagne. It was a typical Evelyn return. Usually he would have taken his father to a film or a theatre, but my father was far from well; he was having injections and running a steady temperature. Instead Evelyn gave him a copy of *1066 and All That*.

I arrived on April 1st; though my flat in Chelsea was unlet I went to my parents' house in North End Road. Evelyn was in partial residence. It was Holy Week and that night he was leaving for retreat at Stonyhurst. My father wrote in his diary, 'Alec home from U.S.A. looking very thin and tired and most charming.' I am not surprised that to my father, who had not seen me for four months, I should have seemed thin. The previous autumn I had had a shock. I had felt that my shirt collars were somewhat tight. I presumed that the material had shrunk, but I thought I had better make sure, so I consulted my tailor. He showed me the measurements of my waistcoats over the last eighteen months.

There had been a steady increase in girth; thirty-two is a dangerous age. I had played my last game of Rugby football in October 1928. I was no longer subjecting myself to training during the last half of the week. I was taking less exercise and eating more. On a cricket tour that summer, in order to avoid a heavy four-course dinner I had ordered every evening sausages, fried eggs and mashed potatoes, which I had washed down with a couple of pints of beer. The time had come to call a halt. I have seldom eaten a potato since: I have substituted wine for beer. It is not difficult to diet in New York, where most people lunch off a cocktail, a single entrée and a coffee. One of my first acts on my return to England was to carry my old suits round to Savile Row and have them taken in: on the whole over the last forty years I have waged a reasonably successful battle against obesity. I am bald and short; there was no need for me to be fat as well, dearly though I appreciate the pleasures of the table.

My mother kept a diary as well as my father. Hers was simply a record of engagements, but the one diary amplifies the other. It was, she records, the wettest Good Friday for fifty years. Richard Connell had said that he would be interested to see the Bank Holiday Fair on Hampstead Heath. He arrived for lunch on the Monday bearing with him a bouquet of flowers, a transatlantic gesture that touched, as much as it surprised, my mother. On the Tuesday I went back to stay in my own flat. I used in those days to put rings in my diary round the days on which fate accorded me the delights of dalliance. There are rings round the Tuesday and the Thursday.

H. G. Wells said in *The World of William Clissold* that all that was required for the conduct of an affair in London was leisure and convenient premises, and a travelling writer can fit easily into the life of a married woman who does not want to be bothered with the strain and responsibilities of a serious affair but is glad to escape every now and again from her routine to a quiet *oubliette* where she can be cherished and appreciated during a shuttered afternoon. There were at this time two such ladies in my life.

Evelyn and I have never, I hope, failed to express appropriate gratitude for the devoted love that our parents gave us. But I have no doubt that their friends, among themselves, often used to complain about the casual way in which we accepted this devotion. 'They treat their parents' home like a hotel. They turn up when it suits them.' But in point of fact that is how my parents wanted their sons to treat their home. And reading over my father's and my mother's diaries, I cannot feel that we were neglectful. During this period Evelyn took his mother to *City Lights*; to the film *Morocco*, and to lunch at my flat into which he had moved when I went away. I took my mother to see *Bitter Sweet*, Marda Vaune's play *To See Ourselves* and to the Ideal Home Exhibition at Olympia. There was no self-sacrifice involved. We enjoyed our parents' company and they knew we did. My father was not well enough to leave the house during the wet chill weather. He spent the time indoors, correcting the proofs of *One Man's Road* and making out his income return. His fees from Chapman and Hall were £800 and he had earned £163 from writing. It was, he wrote, his lowest return for many years.

How far money went in those days, though no one realised it at the time. My father had no private income. He had no old-age pension. My mother had a minute private income. I question if it was more than £30. She had a hoarding instinct. When Underhill was sold in 1933 and they moved to a flat in Highgate, she opened a Post Office Savings Account. I had no idea that she had done so: nor, I think, had Evelyn. But when she died in 1954 it was found that she had amassed some £640. What a happiness that savings account book must have been to her. She always liked to think that if anyone was in need she could be of help to them. She said to me once in her last years, 'If you or Evelyn wanted some money, I should be so proud if I could lend it to you.' I remembered her having said that when her lawyer and I found a Post Office savings book among her papers. If I had known of it, I might have been tempted to borrow a hundred pounds from her, even though I did not need it. It would have given her such a feeling of being useful. It would have been a kindness to her.

I had the incident of that savings account in mind when I was writing my novel *A Spy in the Family*. One of the characters

41

was an apparent playboy, an amateur golfer who represented a wine firm, a very flimsy and uncertain source of income. He was, however, unknown to everyone, employed in the Government Secret Service. His golf and his wine connection were his 'cover'. He was his mother's favourite and he was in the habit of borrowing money from her which he did not need and which he put in a trust fund for his brother's children. It made his mother very happy to feel that she was of vital importance to him. She loved him for his weakness. Eventually he was offered a government decoration, an M.B.E., for his services to the country; he could then have been the spy who came out of the cold, promoted to an administrative post. But he felt forced to refuse, because it would have broken his mother's heart to learn that she was not so important to him after all, that he had been fooling her.

The incident brought, I believe, the character to life. It is another example of how a novelist puts real incidents and real characters into his books. It is a point that I am planning to elaborate in a few pages time when I talk about the novel on which I settled down to work in Villefranche.

As I said, I took my mother to see *Bitter Sweet*. It was showing at the Golders Green Hippodrome. Peggy Wood was in the lead. I had met her the previous autumn at a party given by Mary Servoss and Erin O'Brien Moore who were then acting in *Street Scene*. When I went to America I let my flat to Mary and Erin, and when their London run ended I saw a lot of them in New York. 'Be sure to give Peggy Wood our love,' they had adjured me.

As the Golders Green Hippodrome was at the foot of the North End Road, I called in there after dinner. I had a cosy chat with Peggy Wood about our mutual friends. She was, she told me, going to Vienna to see a musical, *Victoria and her Hussar*, in which there might be a part for her. She was not looking forward to it, she said. Now that *Bitter Sweet* was over she was in a hurry to get back to her son and husband. 'But the trip'll be fun,' I said.

'I don't know. It's a long way, a night on the boat, then twenty-four hours in a train. Besides I've been to Vienna twice.'

'I've never been there.'

'Why not come along, then?'

'Why don't I?'

'I'm catching the 8.15 from Liverpool Street on Sunday week.'

'I'll be there,' I said.

I was at that time ready to fall in with sudden plans. A month earlier in New York, when *Street Scene* was going to the coast, I had nearly gone there with it. But San Francisco was a very long way – nearly two weeks – from the French Riviera, and I wanted to start work on my new novel. Though I was always ready to change my plans at a moment's notice, I was careful not to break my working schedule. Vienna was a different matter – only a few hours from Villefranche. I could take Vienna in my stride. It was a brief diversion. It might provide useful copy; it would be another setting for a story. It should be fun.

It was, but in an unexpected way. On the Tuesday, after moving into my flat, I booked my ticket to Villefranche via Vienna and set about seeing as many of my friends as I could manage during that short time, with a ring in my pocket diary round the seventh and ninth. I dined with my agent, A. D. Peters; I lunched with my lawyer, E. S. P. Haynes; I gave a small dinner party at the Savile, whose main purpose was to introduce Evelyn to Richard Connell; there were one or two attendant courtiers to act as ballast in case my brother's meeting with Connell was unsuccessful, although in those days Evelyn was far from being the difficult element that he became in the later '50s. The dinner seemed to go well enough and I noticed that after the meal they drew apart in a concentrated duologue. I wondered what they were discussing, as Connell was not a Catholic.

Evelyn was staying the night at the Savile, I returned to North End Road.

Next morning Evelyn rang me up. 'That was a good party,' he said. 'Thank you.'

We discussed it for a moment or two. Then he asked after Connell. 'Do you know his address?' he asked.

'The Connaught Hotel,' I told him.

'If I were you, I should ring up and ask if he's all right.'

'Why?'

'He may be dead.'

'What?'

'He told me he wasn't sleeping. So I offered him my pills. I've just looked in my box. He's taken eight. They're very strong, and he isn't used to them. I should think eight would do the trick.'

But Connell had a sturdy constitution. He survived to write many more stories. Later that day I went to Oxford to see the Willerts and on the Sunday to Guildford to make contact with some other friends with whom I was anxious to re-establish immediate touch. I remember that lunch party because a decanter of port was placed upon the table. After the meal it was set back upon the sideboard. It sent a shiver of apprehension along my nerves. After four months of prohibition I was nervous at the sight of an unemptied decanter. Anything might happen to its precious contents.

I was, in fact, so busy during that week that I hardly had time to reflect on the fact that on the Sunday night I was to start off on a trip to Vienna with a female of high attractions whom I scarcely knew. It was something of a shock, therefore, on the Monday morning to find myself after a turbulent crossing facing her across the breakfast table of a dining car. 'What on earth am I doing here?' I thought. I looked at her, appreciatively. It was the first time I had seen her in the daylight. She was of about my age. Without considerable good looks she could not have become the prima donna that she had: she had a healthy, wholesome look. In spite of the early hour and the rough crossing, she was highly appetising. I knew nothing about her, except what the whole world knew: that she was the daughter of a professor of English; that her husband was John V. A. Weaver, the poet; that she mixed with a highbrow group; was one of the Algonquin's Round Table set; that she was a serious actress; that her great role was in *Candida*. I had heard her discussed as an actress, but never as a human being; she was a very agreeable person: she was witty and good company. But I had no idea what she was like. Yet here I was about to spend four days alone with her in early springtime in the glamorous city of Vienna. It was the kind of situation that I had difficulty in devising for the characters in my stories; it is not easy to find a credible situation in which two youngish people, unattached, or at least with no immediate liens should find themselves alone in a strange city or a beach hotel. Four days; and the first day in a train during which they could get to know each other . . . the very situation for a *Cosmopolitan* short story. How was it going to work out in actuality?

It worked out in a way that no fiction editor would have approved, but was exasperatingly true to life. On the Tuesday morning, almost before it was light, I came out into the corridor with the train slowing down at Vienna, to find that Peggy was having difficulty with her luggage. She had hurt her hand, she said. She had shut it in the door of her compartment.

'When did you do that?'

'Last night.'

'Why didn't you let me know?'

'What could you have done? What could anyone have done?'

'Was it hurting?'

'Yes, quite a lot. But there wasn't anything I could do. I had to wait till I could see a doctor. I cried myself to sleep.'

I cannot think of any conduct less like what you would expect from a theatrical prima donna. Yet I cannot think of any action that was more like Peggy Wood. She was not the person to make a fuss, when making a fuss would not do any good.

Her first act in Vienna was to find a doctor. She returned from his consulting room with the information that she had broken a finger and with her arm in a sling. That settled the problems of the magazine short story situation. There is no more effective chaperone than an arm stretched across a bosom in a sling. During our four days in Vienna we laid the basis for a friendship that has lasted forty years.

Those four days in Vienna were indeed among the very best in this year that is the one which I would most gratefully relive. We saw *Victoria and her Hussar*. It came to London in the autumn. Whether it ever reached New York I do not know. If it did, I do not believe it was a great success. I remember chiefly about it – I was watching it in German which I cannot speak – a wonderful duet sung by Oscar Denes, a large plump romantic creature, and just the right itsy-bitsy Poppet to be a foil for him. I did not feel it was the right medium for Peggy Wood because the heroine was a married woman whose husband has been kind and loyal, but whom she leaves for the sake of another man because she loves him more. Somehow I did not see that as the right role for the star of *Bitter Sweet*. Today that might seem a ridiculous objection but divorce was not quite so universally condoned in 1931.

For the most part in Vienna we were straight-forward sight-seers. Schonbrun, the gardens, the galleries, all that. We also, through Peggy, had some social contacts. Larry Larue was then the local *Herald Tribune* representative; at the party that he gave for Peggy, I met John Gunther, then on the threshold of his long series of successes. Larry Larue's current wife became later Maureen Shirer, whose guest I was often to be after the second war in Princeton at the Music Box. A great deal started, in fact, during that five day visit in Vienna: later I became a very good friend of Peggy's husband, John V. A. Weaver. Once we went down together for a working holiday to the Easton Court Hotel, of which I shall be writing in a future chapter. Peggy herself was soon to be back in England, acting in the musical *The Cat and the Fiddle*. Peggy was, as she is, a person of great prominence in the theatre on both sides of the Atlantic. Friendship with her opened many doors for me.

I can remember little of what was discussed at Larry Larue's party. Most of the guests were foreign journalists, and there must have been some talk of the fact that earlier in the week, on the Sunday, Spain in the first free elections for eight years had voted for the Republicans, and on the Tuesday King Alfonso had gone into exile.

When I read of it in the *Continental Daily Mail*, my first thought had been 'What will Ruth think of this?' She had been in Spain when Alec Moore had been the American Ambassador. They had been great friends. There is even an oblique reference to her in *The Sun Also Rises*; she had moved on the fringe of the court circles. She was a friend of Primo Rivera. Her eight months there had been a high point of glamour. Now the Spain that she had loved had vanished, had become an anachronism.

How strange, I had thought, that a mere election could turn a king off a throne. How lucky England was to have a constitution and a limited monarchy that stood outside the hustings. It seemed ridiculous that the traditions and inherited culture of a sovereign state could be at the mercy of the whim of a popular vote. But the event had no personal message for me at the time. I did not foresee that in five years' time a revolution would have broken out that would split England into two opposing factions, that would divide friends and families, that would cause enmities and feuds that would only end when Britain was under the impact of a menace to its very existence that had its roots in Alfonso's hurried exodus from Madrid.

If any of Larue's other guests were more prescient than I, I do not know. Perhaps they were, but, as far as I can remember, most of the people there were anxious to hear the latest news of New York from Peggy and myself.

V

On Saturday April 18th, I caught a train for Villefranche. During the last eighteen months Villefranche had become a home for me. I saw it first in 1925. I was on my way back to England after two weeks in Florence. Tired by an uncomfortable night in a second-class carriage in a crowded train, I was looking with casual eyes through the carriage window when, suddenly, there it lay below me, the little land-locked harbour with the greyhound cruisers at anchor, the wide-curved waterfront, the tall painted houses, yellow, pink and blue, high-storeyed with green shutters and iron balconies. Very lovely and tranquil and self-contained it looked under the blue sky, under the amber sunlight, against the grey-brown background of its hills. In the same way that I fell in love with Tahiti at first sight, I fell in love with Villefranche. 'I'll be back soon,' I thought. That was my first impression and I have yet to be betrayed by first impressions; of places as of people.

It was not till the late summer of 1929, however, that I did get back. At the end of the cricket season I had a novel to finish. Berta Ruck was in Villefranche with her sons, also finishing a novel. She was staying at the Welcome Hotel. Why did I not come down and finish mine there, too? Why not indeed? I stayed a month. By the time the month was up, I was in love, not only with Villefranche.

She was seventeen years old. She was called Cécile. Under the supervision of her parents she and her sister Doleen ran the Garden Bar, in the narrow Rue du Poilu that runs parallel with the waterfront, at the start of the network of narrow streets that, cutting back into the rock, clamber up the hillside to the Corniche Road. With her hair piled high upon her forehead, her cheeks full and her chin pointed, her head was shaped like a heart. Her black hair, drawn tightly behind the ears, fell in curls upon her shoulders. Her unplucked eyebrows were bright with brilliantine. Her eyelashes were long and curled. Her teeth were very small and white: her mouth unrouged and smiling. As she leant across the zinc bar of her café against a background of many-coloured bottles, she soon came to symbolise the whole spirit of Villefranche for me.

I visited her bar most evenings. I say I fell in love with her and there is no other label for the emotion that she evoked: and for that matter still evokes; I always visit her when I go to Nice. She is now married – for the second time – to a dentist. She has an elegant flat in the Avenue Mirabeau. She is a grandmother, and I take the granddaughters to the cinema and to a café for an ice-cream afterwards. We are very close. But from the very start I realised that there could be no unplatonic outcome to our *amitié*. She was chaperoned to an extent that seemed excessive, even in the France of the 1920s. Her parents were Italian. Cécile had been born in Arezzo, and perhaps a distrust of foreigners accentuated her father's vigilance, but Cécile herself did not resent it. She was, herself, extremely modest. The parents had a small property in the mountains, whose produce contributed largely to the family's support. The narrow square at the back of the Welcome is today a garage. But it is still called *Place du Marché* and in 1931 it really was a market; her parents had a stall there, which was run by the younger sister, Doleen, a red-head, a very much more outgoing person. Cécile's life on the other hand was bounded by the four walls of her bar. Her family house was fifty or so yards higher up, and for days on end she would not walk further than that fifty yards. Once a week she would go to have her hair dressed on the Corniche Road. Occasionally at four o'clock in the afternoon, she would descend to the pâtisserie in front of the market place for a cup of chocolate.

I once from my bedroom in the hotel took a film of her with a ciné-Kodak. It was in April: the day was chilly. She was wearing a dark coat and skirt. Her hands were thrust into her coat pockets, her head bent forward. She gave the impression of someone hurrying through a hostile city. Which in a way she was. She felt unsure of herself outside her bar; in that dark, cool room she could relax. She was among friends, in her own setting. She was like a princess holding court. She had a smile for everyone who came there, for the fishermen from the quay, the masons from the upper town, the Chasseurs Alpins from the barracks, sailors on leave, tourists such as myself; we were all her guests. She moved like a hostess from one table to another, talking now to this one, then to that. Occasionally she would offer an apéritif to a special friend. She herself never drank, except when she was thirsty; and then it was a Vichy or a peppermint. When the fleet was in, and hospitable clients grew insistent, she had recourse to a brown unlabelled bottle. 'It is my own liqueur,' she would say, and charge four francs for it. It contained, of course, water and brown sugar.

I had written to Cécile after I had left Villefranche. In the spring I returned after a sea trip to East Africa. In the summer again I had returned for a three week visit. We had exchanged letters and postcards during my winter in New York. My heart beat quickly, as the train came out from the tunnel after Beaulieu and I saw the cluster of houses along the waterfront and the blank wall facing me with its Dubonnet sign. Cécile knew that I was coming, but she did not know the exact day. How excited she would be when I came into the bar. 'And this time I'll be able to tell her,' I thought, 'that I'm to stay two months.' Which was about the time it would take me, I believed, to write the novel that I had in mind.

One of the first questions that novelists are always asked is 'Do you know the end before you start? Do you change your mind as you go along? Don't your characters sometimes take control?'

I have answered those questions with a simile. 'It is like going for a walk,' I say, 'you see a house on a hill. It is fifteen miles away. You walk at four miles an hour. You will have to take a rest every now and again. You can expect to take four hours. You cannot be sure, though, of the exact road that you will follow. There is a good deal of dead ground between the house on the distant hill and the point where you are standing. There may be a valley that will force you to make a detour: or there may be a charming orchard where you will want to linger: there may be a ruin worth examining. You cannot foresee your exact route.

But you know where you are headed. You know how long it will take you to cover fifteen miles.'

That is the answer that I give from the lecture platform, and it is mainly true, with this one modification that I have usually found that I break down after I have been writing for three weeks. The story stops. I have to take a rest. I may have begun in the wrong place; or I may have got one of the characters out of focus; in *Island in the Sun* for instance, I started by making Julian Fleury, rather than his son Maxwell, spurred into jealousy by detecting in the lavatory the smell of a strange cigarette. It would have been a fatal mistake, because a man of over fifty would not have been jealous in that way about the indiscretions of a woman of his own age, his wife for thirty years. At any rate that kind of husband. He would have felt pity, a need to help, 'Poor old girl, I'll have to see her through this mess.'

I took a six week rest and then started in from a fresh angle. That has happened with nearly all my novels. Once I have got my second wind, the simile of the house on the hill holds good. I know where I am bound and I know how long it will take me to arrive – a 70,000 or a 90,000 or a 130,000 word book.

When I started on this novel at Villefranche, I anticipated a book of around 130,000 words, and I anticipated writing around 15,000 words a week. My prophecy was fulfilled. I began writing on April 20th. I was due to leave on June 24th in order to get back to England to see the first day of the Lord's Test Match. I finished the book on June 20th. This book was exceptional in the one respect that I did not have the traditional breakdown at the end of the third week. I have kept the manuscript. It is written by hand on squared French *cahiers*, and the pace does not falter. I could not have foreseen that I would break my rule, and carry on without a pause; but then in spite of my experience I have always been surprised when that break has come. I have always started off calmly confident that I will stride straight to the house on the far hill.

I have never written a book with greater confidence and greater enjoyment. And it was as much as anything the enjoyment in its writing that made 1931 such a happy year for me. The book was published in England in late November and in New York in January, and throughout the remainder of the year, I had the warm feeling of a worthwhile job completed. I cheerfully anticipated a warm public reception for it. Nor was I disappointed: the book was well received and its sales in view of the monetary problems with which the world was then afflicted were far from unsatisfactory. Yet to me, now, in retrospect, it seems that in my fifteenth year as a novelist I was making as many mistakes as the most modest tyro.

I was planning a novel that would both present a picture of contemporary New York and tell the story of my romance with Ruth. My introduction to New York had been in its own way as profound an experience as the love affair in which 'my honour rooted in dishonour stood.' In each case I had been introduced to a world of new sensations. In neither case could I be the same person again.

In order to write this story I had to make the hero a man with a great deal of leisure. It had to be possible for him to cross oceans when his inamorata raised her finger: and if the situation became intolerable he could solve it, temporarily, by catching a ship to England. Moreover, if the book was to present contemporary New York it had to be possible for the hero to spend a good deal of time there. It was hard to see how the hero could be anything but a novelist. I could not make him an international playboy because a reader cannot be interested in a man who does nothing, in whose life nothing is at stake. The hero must be positive. He must stand for something, strive for something. It is not till he has been shown in terms of his ambition that the reader is prepared to be interested in his domestic trials. If not heroic, he must show resolution in a crisis. A boardroom can be as ruthless as a battlefield, the floating of a company as hazardous as the launching of a frigate; a group of directors watching the ticking of a tape machine can be shown as the twentieth-century equivalent of the last Spartans at Thermopylae. The hero has to be a man of action: he has to have a profession. And who but a novelist could get himself involved in the way that I had with Ruth. That was my first mistake; for there is one infallible rule for the writing of fiction: 'Never choose a novelist for your hero.' I was given that advice by Ralph Straus when my first novel was in the press and I myself in my nineteenth year. I have followed it dutifully except on this one occasion.

The novelist is a fate-favoured person; at a first glance he would seem the perfect hero for a novel. He is as free as air. He can work where he likes, when he likes, under conditions of his own choosing. No one bosses him around; he carries his office with him. The circumference of his world is drawn by the radius of his interests. It is indeed possible that he might be the good hero of a picaresque novel; travelling around with a letter of credit and letters of introduction, meeting a variety of adventures, amatory and otherwise; yet it will be hard to present him as anything but a playboy, because it is impossible to present his writing as anything more serious than a profitable hobby.

In itself writing is undramatic. Flaubert's picture of himself seated at a window in a dressing gown watching the Seine flow past, waiting for the inevitable word, is a caricature of the average novelist, but it bears a recognisable resemblance. No career could involve less drama. His problems are worked out in privacy; they involve no personal relationships; there are no directors to be conciliated, exposed or shouldered out of office; no refractory cabinets to be cajoled or over-ridden. His interviews with publishers and editors are of a social nature. His battles are fought out in his own mind.

Yet altogether apart from 'the agonies of composition' a novelist does have to be very ruthless in the conduct of his profession. Many, many Septembers ago, a lady to whom I had been paying not unassiduous court during a London season told me that her doctor had warned her against the rigours of an English winter. He had recommended the South of France. She had been lent a flat in Cannes. Why should I not find the equivalent of 'a willow cabin at her gate'? She would be alone there. I could spend the mornings on my manuscript. We would have the rest of the day to ourselves. She suggested that my patience and devotion would not go unrewarded.

It was what I appeared to have been praying for all through

the summer. But I had made plans to take a long trip to the West Indies. I was curious to see Martinique. A French island as far north of the line as was Tahiti south should present interesting aspects of comparison. An instinct told me that it was important for my writing that I should go there. I set my trip there in the balance against a winter on the Côte d'Azur. It would, of course, be wonderful to be alone with a person to whom I, at the age of thirty, was considerably attracted. But what should I do the rest of the time? Cannes out of the season? November is a rainy month. Gambling bored me. I did not like frittering away money that I had earned with difficulty. There would be no amusing parties. The only foreigners around would be impoverished expatriates who could not afford to get away. There was my manuscript, of course, but it only needed another month. What should I do when it was finished? Wait for ideas to come? It would not, of course, have been all that dreary. I have more than once, since the Second War, spent October, November and December in the South of France. Cannes out of the season is infinitely better than most places in it: and on this occasion there would have been the dividend of a long-sought romance: but an inner voice was counselling me not to cancel my sailing to Martinique. And that inner voice – the daemon that guided Socrates – should never be denied.

It was for me as a novelist a genuine moment of crisis, but one that it would not be possible to present convincingly in a novel. Many, many years later, not so very long ago in fact, the lady whom I had not joined in Cannes asked me the real reason for my negligence. 'You can surely tell me the truth now.'

I told her the truth. A look of incredulity came into her face. 'You went there to get material for a book? I thought you had a real reason. I thought that that girl of Margaret's was getting troublesome. I know she wanted you as a son-in-law! I've always wondered. You say you went to get material for a book. I've never heard anything so silly in my life.'

That is, I believe, how any reader would feel about the issue: how could the man who has to spend forty-nine weeks a year at an office desk feel any sympathy for one who has to choose between the alternatives of a winter accompanied by a love affair in the South of France and a five month cruise among the Caribbean islands. No one, he would think, has the right to so good a life. And as for the youngish woman, with a wandering eye, whose husband returns home each evening from the city exhausted by the tapping of the typewriter and the screeching of the telephone, whose potential admirers are equally imprisoned within the walls of a forty hour week, who must so often think, 'If only I could really be alone with him: the only consolation is that he must be thinking that every bit as much himself.' What contempt would she not have for the hero who lets up a chance like that.

Yet the fact remains incontestably that that daemon, that inner voice, gave me the correct advice. That trip was decisive, in a way that I could not have foreseen. I went to the West Indies, so that I could draw comparisons between Tahiti and Martinique, but before I had been there three weeks those comparisons had become unimportant. I had become absorbed in the West Indians themselves, in their history, their problems and their future. I had found in fact the subject I had been looking for. Now, at the end of my writing life, I am known, and am happy to be known, as the author of *Island in the Sun*. Had I spent the winter of 1928–29 in dalliance, my writing career might have petered out in the 1930s and I might have lacked the faith to start again after the Second War. The 'daemon' is always right.

There is only one way in which a novelist can be used as a central character and that is as the 'I' of the narrative, as a *raisonneur*. This method has been perfected by Maugham in *The Razor's Edge*. He also used it in *Cakes and Ale*, though there he does make himself in his scenes with Rosie a protagonist: he does so, however, with great caution, standing outside himself, seeing himself from a distance of many years. In *The Razor's Edge* he is consistently the observer and there he takes full advantage of the novelist's power to travel; to be part of a great many different lives. In the course of his account of other people's histories, he tells us a great deal about himself. I have used this device in my novel *The Fatal Gift*.

In *So Lovers Dream* I was on the wrong tack from the start. I should have realised this. But I wanted to write the book.

In my partial autobiography, *The Early Years of Alec Waugh*, I told the story of my romance with Ruth. I could do that then because Ruth and her husband were both dead, and though I did not mention her by name, because his daughters are still alive, it would not have mattered at this late day if Ruth could be identified in Pebble Beach. But in 1931 it was very important that no one in California should say 'So that's what those two were about, is it?' I had to find, therefore, equivalent situations for the real ones. I placed their American meetings in New York instead of in California, and I chose Villefranche as an alternative for Tahiti.

The parallel was reasonably close. In Tahiti, Ruth and her husband had rented a bungalow in Paea, forty or so kilometres from Papeete. I was staying in a guest house half way between Paea and Papeete: There were cabins along the beach. A friend of Ruth's was staying at the guest house, her husband was on a pearl hunt in the Paumutos. It was logical that Ruth should visit her every fourth or fifth night, and during the day she could often look in for a short talk, a drink or a cup of coffee. I did not have a car, for the simple reason that I did not know how to drive one. In London, in the early '20s, a Londoner in my position did not own a car. My brother Evelyn did not learn to drive until his second marriage. But he was never at ease at the wheel and soon abandoned the experiment. I had therefore to wait at my beach hotel, hour after hour, day after day, waiting for the chance of Ruth's being free. I was a prisoner 'like one of those shop girls in a Victorian novel,' I told her, 'who were kept by their protector in a villa in Acacia Road, and in the days before there were telephones had to wait till their lord and master could escape from a Parliamentary Debate.' The parallel was not inexact. There were telephones in Tahiti, but every one was on a party line: I could not risk them. It was an intolerable situation. I had no alternative to a return to London. Though I was heartbroken at the thought of leaving Ruth, I counted the days till my ship's sailing.

For the purposes of my novel, I could find an equivalent in the

South of France, with me staying in the Welcome, while Ruth had a villa on Cap Ferrat. There, as in Tahiti, it would be my role to wait until Ruth was free: till her grey-green Chevrolet swung into the square, and a small urchin would hurry down to the beach in search of me, 'l'Américaine est ici' he would say. I had intended to call the book *l'Américaine*.

That situation was psychologically an equivalent for the one in the South Seas, and though I was careful not to make the husband in any way a portrait of Ruth's, I could make him a psychological equivalent. I made him a New Yorker in his middle forties, a prosperous business man: hearty, an extrovert, making himself the centre figure of any group. He was not exactly aggressive, but you were conscious of him all the time. He might have been called by a European 'a typical American'. He was not quite a stock character, because I had the husband so much in mind that he was real to me. He disarmed the hero of the book just as I had been disarmed by his taking control of every situation, by always picking up the check, by refusing to let me be the host. When my hero had invited the pair to Villefranche for lunch a servant was sent over at the last moment to say that two friends had unexpectedly turned up, and would Gordon mind a change of plan; would he instead come over to Cap Ferrat? A chauffeur was beside the car; there was no alternative to acceptance. In just that way in Tahiti had I been forced to accept a minor role, yet no one reading the book in California would have taken it as a portrait of Ruth's husband who was a writer, who had been to Yale, who was a scholar as well as an athlete. He had the background of a well known ancestor, whose despatches when he was ambassador to Louis XVI were familiar to any student of history. I handled that piece of portraiture satisfactorily.

But in the portrait of Ruth – I called her Faith – my resolve to make her unrecognisable made her shadowy. In my autobiography I have drawn what is I hope a vivid picture of her. She was described as:

. . . small and trim, her hair was brown with a glint of red in it. I do not think that she was pretty, but she had the most beautiful voice I have ever heard. She could light up a party, not by 'stealing the show', but by making the others more alive, so that they talked better, laughed more readily, contributed more to the general fund of gaiety. She was a dramatic person and she had led a dramatic life. She was one of the first Americans to fly an aeroplane, and one of the seven or eight American women to be given an Army commission in the first war, in her case to train pilots. She had driven racing cars professionally. She had written scripts for motion pictures. In Spain she had remarked unguardedly that bullfighting did not look so difficult. Someone retorted 'You try to do it': she took up the challenge, trained, learned the technique and having killed her bull, went to fashionable parties in Madrid in her matador costume. She was wild, very wild, with an at times ungovernable temper. But she was capable of an extreme sweetness. She could make you feel as though you were living in an enchanted country where the air was softer, the scent of the flowers richer, the plumage of the birds more bright.

That is how I described her in my autobiography. But the Faith of *So Lovers Dream* was not in the least like that: she was quiet, withdrawn, a shrine, a shrouded goddess. There is no reason why such a character should not be an effective heroine of a novel, but in this case, since I had Ruth in mind all the time, and I was making this shadowy creature do the things and say the things that Ruth had done and said, she did not ring true. A novel is an artificial creation, and real life incidents are out of place in it. Theodore Benson's mother placed in one of her novels a proposal of marriage in which the suitor quoted from Browning. A critic complained that no suitor would quote from Browning, in that way. Theodora's mother retorted that two of the men who had proposed to her had quoted Browning. But that does not prove the critic wrong. To him a proposal of marriage with a quotation from Browning did not ring true. In my opinion the best way of putting a real character into a book is to devise an entirely imaginary setting and series of incidents and let the character behave and speak as you know he or she would. I did this with the heroine of my novel *The Mule on the Minaret*! There I had a direct portrait of a woman I knew extremely well, so well that I knew precisely how she would behave and what she would say in the circumstances I had devised.

In *So Lovers Dream* I followed this practice in the case of a minor character. I mentioned earlier that I had had a romance while I was in New York. I also mentioned that on my return to my flat in London, two days in my pocket diary were ringed. For this purpose I transferred my American friend from New York to London. She was a New Englander, in her middle 20s, who had a rebel and a truant nature. Breaking loose from the rigid circumstances of her home, and hitch-hiking across America, she wrote a description of her trip in the course of which she had two love affairs – one of them with a truck driver – and published it under the name Barbara Starke, with the title *Touch and Go*. In the preface which I wrote for the English edition, I described it as the most outspoken book ever written by a young girl. She was the greatest fun – independent, light-hearted, undemanding.

If any readers of these pages will look up *So Lovers Dream* in their local library and turn to pages 74–87, they will see how I transported her from New York to London. In my opinion they are fourteen of the best pages I have ever written. Several of my English friends asked me who she was. They refused to believe that it was an imaginary portrait. 'There's something in it that rings true,' they said, and they were sceptical when I told them that I did have an American girl in mind. 'You're being very noble,' they said. 'You are protecting a woman's honour.' But Barbara had no doubt that it was a portrait of herself. She was, in fact, delighted with it. As an example of the different use to which two writers can put a similar experience, may I refer to Eric Linklater's *Magnus Merriman*, in which the American girl is photographically like Barbara, whom he met in Scotland in the summer of 1932?

The story that I wrote in Villefranche had, therefore, two strikes against it: a hero in whose problems, because he appeared a playboy, the reader could not be expected to take a warm personal interest, and a shadowy heroine. At the same time it was written with considerable emotion: it has some good descriptive passages, and some lively minor characters. It is not a bad book by any means.

I should have enjoyed the writing of it wherever I had been, even in The White Horse at Shenley, and in winter time. But the Welcome Hotel in early summer was perfect for such a project. It is one of the Inns of Legend. In the first edition of Scott Fitzgerald's *Tender is the Night* there are pen and ink sketches at the head of every chapter. There is one of the Villefranche waterfront. The Welcome is the hotel at which the lovers broke their drive from Juan to Monte Carlo and there is an account of a lady of the town waving goodbye to her French sailor as he leaves to join his battleship. There are descriptions of the Welcome in Glenway Westcott's *Goodbye Wisconsin* and his recent *Images of Truth*. In front of the Welcome, the old Tribunal de Peche which was never used as a tribunal in my day has been converted by Jean Cocteau into a chapel dedicated to the patron saint of fishermen. In the lounge of the hotel hangs one of the sketches that Cocteau made for his frescoes. It is inscribed *à mon cher Welcome où j'ai passé les meilleurs de ma vie*. In the 1920s Paul Morand and Monroe Wheeler had villas on the slopes above the harbour. They both used the Welcome as a club. Across the bay Somerset Maugham was sumptuously installed at the Villa Mauresque. When friends of his arrived at Villefranche, they would announce their presence at the Welcome by note or telephone. It was not unlike the routine in a small West Indian Island when you sign the book at Government House and await an appropriate invitation. Indeed there was something of an island's atmosphere about Villefranche in the 1930s. You were cut off from the main current of Riviera life. Fast trains, the *rapides*, rarely stopped there. If you wanted to go into Nice and did not have a car – and at that time Welcome Hotel patrons did not ordinarily have cars – you had to climb the hill to the lower Corniche Road, to what is still called the Octroi (though it is many years since any customs dues have been collected there) and take a trolley. That trolley was like a ferry connecting an island with the mainland. This feeling of being apart from the main traffic of the coast gave Villefranche a particular appeal for the writer and the painter. You could concentrate upon your work with the weeks passing in a day-to-day eventlessness.

From the railway line, the waterfront looks very much the same as it did today, when I saw it first fifty years ago: but the entire inside of the Welcome has been rebuilt and an extra floor been added: a row of restaurants stretches along the Quay: a road has been carried to the beach below the railway line; there is a constant flow of cars. The young girls no longer stroll along the harbourside in couples, with their long black hair hanging low upon their necks, while the young men seated on the steps eye them enviously. The harbourside is now given over to the tourist: the young people have moved to the upper town.

My life followed a smooth routine. I would wake around six, with the ripples of the sea reflected by the sunlight on my ceiling. I would stroll to the pebbled beach below the railway line. The waterfront stopped, by what is still called the Réserve and there was a pool where the fishermen kept their lobsters. I climbed up a flight of steps that still exists to the road leading to the station, and from which a flight of steps then as now leads to the beach. Probably there would be a fisherman seated on the rocks. While I swam, a train would come through from Italy. It was one of the few main trains that stopped at Villefranche. The wagon-lits windows would be tightly shuttered, but grubby unshaven Italians would lean out of the third class windows. By the time I had finished my swim the market would have opened and I would buy, from Doleen's store, some figs to accompany my breakfast on the terrace at one of its three or four round blue-topped tables. The *Continental Daily Mail* arrived a day late from Paris, and I would read it as I sipped my coffee. In England it was an exceedingly wet summer; *The Times* at the end of the year described it as 'dour beyond belief'—the second of the three bad summers that produced such negligible wine on the banks of the Medoc and on the golden slopes that rise south of Dijon. Day after day, I would read that not a ball had been bowled on any first-class cricket ground in England. The news gave a zest to my appreciation of the good things that lay about me. How lucky I was to be here not there; how wise I had been to take full advantage of a writer's luck.

By eight o'clock I had started my morning's writing. The hotel was barely a quarter full. Most of the other guests preferred to take breakfast in their rooms, but a young American couple, Kathy and Walker Ellis, who were staying at the Réserve – the couple about whom Glenway Westcott wrote in *Images of Truth* – often came across for a second cup of coffee. Their presence did not disturb me. My concentration was so complete that I could join in their intermittent gossip. They contributed to the morning's peace, just as did the children who came to look over my shoulder at my manuscript and surreptitiously purloin a lump of sugar: they were part of the morning scene. The nets stretched out to dry upon the cobbles, the women at work on them, the boats awash against their moorings; the men cleaning their boats; and then at about nine fifteen the *facteur* coming round with the morning's mail, were all so many figures on a frieze: they no more disturbed my concentration than the headlines in the *Daily Mail*. The continuing slump on the Stock Market, the rising number of unemployed in England belonged to another world.

I have always worked to a fixed formula of so many words a day. In those days I did three thousand. Sometimes I would wake sleepless at 2 a.m. Rather than read myself back to sleep, I would return to my manuscript and write till my eyes felt heavy. I used to think it was a good sign when a manuscript woke me up. It showed that my subconscious was working while I slept. I was never woken by a piece of hackwork, a magazine serial would stay on the surface of my mind. The number of words that I had written during the night was added to my scheduled stretch for the next day. I would think as I walked to the beach for my first swim, 'only 2,250 more words to do.'

It may seem unromantic to break off a piece of narrative in the middle of a scene. The public likes to believe in the white hot frenzy of inspiration. Anthony Trollope lost his public for thirty years, by explaining how he worked with his watch in front of him every morning, and a fixed task set so that he would finish one novel at 7.21 and begin its successor at 7.23. Browning did not send up his stock by admitting that he never sat down to his desk without reluctance or rose from it without relief. But most professional writers have to resort to some artificial means to keep the machinery of production oiled. Arnold Bennett advised the novelist to leave himself an easy piece of writing to do next morning, so that he could get back quickly into the last day's mood; and to resist the temptation to finish off an exciting scene the night before. He would end up exhausted, and have next day to make a new beginning. The first paragraph, the 'lead' of any piece of writing is the most difficult. Michael Arlen when he was writing *The Green Hat* used each morning to copy out the last half page that he had written the night before. This put him back into the mood. Each writer evolves the method that suits him best. I have enjoyed the sight of my handwriting moving down to the foot of the page. The manuscript of *So Lovers Dream* is the only one that I retained when my home in England was broken up and my library sold. It is bound in half dark-blue calf. I kept it because it reminded me of happy days and I often turn its pages to be reminded of them. It was also my one uniform manuscript, written throughout on French cahiers with ruled lines; when I started on the last half I wrote on every other line instead of every fourth line, 47 lines a page at 23 words a line made 1,100 words a page. At this point I switched to a 3,300 word a day schedule. It is clearly legible but I do not think any typist today would undertake such a manuscript; once again, twelve years later, I was to write in an equally compressed form. When I was in the Middle East as a serving officer and limited to six airmail letter cards a week, I managed to cram a 2,000 word short story on to a single card. If anyone would be interested to see one of my MSS they can find them in the Boston University Libraries and in the University of Texas.

I wrote about 500 words an hour. By eleven o'clock it was time for my morning swim. Sometimes when I could persuade the Walker Ellis's to join me, I would hire a row boat and cross to the beach, *passable*, on Cap Ferrat. There was real sand there and the water was clean. With so many ships anchoring in the harbour,

I cannot but believe that the water under the railway bridge was highly septic. I remember once that after a heavy cloudburst a cow drowned in Nice was washed into the harbour, where it remained untended for half a week.

In those days during the season – and the winter season continued into the middle of May – there were no demi-pension rates at the Welcome, so that for Scottish reasons I took most of my meals at the hotel. The Welcome liked one to be punctual. Lunch was announced for half past twelve. By two o'clock I was back at my desk to tackle the remainder of my daily task. I still, over forty years later, follow the same routine. But I write fewer words, 2,000 if it is a novel, 1,500 if it is a biography. I have only an hour to put in after lunch: then I take a siesta. That in 1931 I did not do; not even when I was in the tropics. Young people always wake from a siesta with a rough mouth and a heavy head. The young cannot take the short, ten minute nap that the elderly find so refreshing. They sleep for ninety minutes. The relief of the siesta is one of the recompenses that old age brings. I began to savour it during the Second War when I was in the Middle East.

When Berta Ruck was staying in the Welcome in 1929, she insisted on my accompanying her on a strenuous walk, after an hour's pause to digest our lunch. It was very good for me. Once we climbed to the Hotel Pyramides. I look at the hotel now and wonder if I could ever have reached it, without Berta Ruck to goad me into exercise. I worked quietly till my day's stint was finished, then I went to my final bathe. The waterfront was in shadow, but the water had taken on the mauvish glaze that had made Homer call it wine-coloured, and the sun's last colours were reflected on to the tall straight houses. I would lie on the shingled beach letting the heat soak into my bones.

Today there is a terrace outside the Welcome dining-room, and during dinner there is a procession of musicians; there is a flame swallower; there is a trick cyclist who performs all along the coast and who has appeared in a number of Riviera films. But then it was all very quiet along the harbour, except when a ship was in. It was restful sitting in front of the Welcome bar with a *fine* maison and a coffee until it was time to go up to the Garden Bar, to play dice or cards, or dance to the gramophone. I would content myself with a single glass of wine there – I was resolved to wake fresh on the next day. The streets would be silent when I walked back to the Hotel; I would lean on my balcony window; the humped shadow of Cap Ferrat would be veiled and poetic in the dusk: the red light on the edge of the port would flicker on and off. All was quiet. What peace, I would think. What beauty; and it was reassuring to look at the cahier on my writing table, waiting for my assault on it next morning.

That was how it was, day after day, week after week, with the variety offered by my discovering every fifth or sixth morning that I was not in the mood for work. I needed a change and would spend the day in Nice: it was a pleasant break after five days on the island that Villefranche had become for me. There was the effort of the climb up to the Octroi where the trolley stopped. It was a slow rattling journey past Mont Boron, and that fantastic pink castellated 'folly' that had been built by an eccentric Englishman in the days when the English believed that the Riviera was as much their's as Brighton. And it was good to see the port of the old town where the 'Ile de Beauté' took off for Corsica. I have always vowed that I would take it but something has always intervened to stop me. Even in 1969 when the P.E.N. Club held their Congress in Menton. There are some admirable restaurants along the port – particularly Garrac's which has two stars in Michelin and the best *bouillabaisse sans langouste* that I know. It was pleasant looking at the smart shops in the Avenue de Verdun, and sauntering along the Promenade des Anglais. I did not make it an expensive day; I would lunch at one of the Alsatian restaurants; there was one, there still is, just where the trolley stopped. I might have a choucroute, or I might be content with a long ham roll, which I would wash down with a stein of light yellow beer. There was a Turkish Bath there with a domed roof, run by a very fat lame masseur; there was in the rue d'Alger an accommodating establishment that displayed blue films. The room in which they were shown was lined with mirrors; I found that the films were more inflammatory when I watched their reflections in the mirror. The frames of the mirrors cut across the film, but a greater sense of reality was obtained. I had the feeling of being a 'voyeur'. After the Turkish Bath or the film, whichever I patronised, I would go to Voyade's, a tea shop in the Place Masséna, which still exists though the shop is now half its size.

A half day in Nice was the recreation I needed from my manuscript, yet even so the best moment of it all was the slow walk down the steep streets from the Octroi, while the slow healing tides of peace stole over me.

Nowadays it is in November that hotels and restaurants along the Riviera close. November is the rainy month. Most tourists would prefer to be somewhere else, or else to be preparing at home for Christmas. But in 1931, the Victorian tradition of the season that ended after Easter still persisted and, in early May, the Welcome decided to close down. It was a disappointment for me, but I was fortunate in having my friend Eldred Curwen installed in a villa in Antibes. He invited me to spend a fortnight with him.

VI

It was with Eldred Curwen that I started in December 1928 for the trip through the West Indies that was to prove so determining a factor in my writing, and during that trip Eldred became closer to me than any man has ever been. He died in September 1955 and the world has not been the same place since.

We met in April 1924. I had spent ten days with Luke and Renée Hansard in their villa above Cannes in Mougins and I was on my way to Florence to spend ten days with C. K. Scott Moncrieff who had a flat there. I arrived early in the morning, shortly after eight. My taximan had no change for a thousand lire note. I had some difficulty, as I did not speak Italian, in obtaining admittance. When I did, it was to find a young, small, but well-built, red-haired young man in his bath. He was astonished by what he took to be my request to lend him 1,000 lire. Eventually we came to understand each other, and the taximan went on his way contented. The young man was Eldred Curwen. Scott-Moncrieff had gone to Montecatini because a great friend of his, a Colonel Evans, had needed to take the waters. He had written to me at Mougins explaining this, but the posts to Mougins were erratic, and the letter had not reached me. Eldred had only happened to be in the flat because he had been afraid that he had caught a dose of clap and had come to Florence to see a doctor. I had never heard of him, he had barely heard of me. I do not know what would have happened if he had not been in the flat. I should never have thought of Moncrieff being in Montecatini. 'We had better cable him that you are here,' Eldred suggested. 'I have a doctor's appointment in the afternoon. We can catch the evening train.'

That is how our friendship started. Knowing nothing of each other we had to spend a whole day together in each other's company. It was a strange day for both of us. Eldred, fearing that he might have clap, did not want to have wine at lunch until he had received his doctor's clearance. I do not mind drinking by myself, but two men get on cordial terms much quicker if they can split a bottle. He was shy of telling me why he was not drinking wine. He assumed that as I had written several books I would want an educational morning, so we went round the Uffizi gallery. After lunch we went to the Pitti Palace. At four o'clock he had his appointment with the doctor: he had had his preliminary interview the day before and was now awaiting the outcome of his tests. The tests were negative. He came out of the consulting room with a wide grin. 'It's all right,' he said. 'No need to worry. Let's have a Negroni.' It was my first visit to Italy. I did not know what a Negroni was. 'It's a gin and vermouth,' he said. 'You'll like it.' Four thirty on a sunny afternoon did not seem the best time for a drink like that. But I made no opposition. Two sips of the Negroni, and Eldred became the lively indefatigable companion that he was to remain for the next thirty years. He then told me what had been on his mind all the morning. It was not surprising that he had been indifferent company and picture galleries are not perhaps the best setting for the growth of intimacy.

We were together for ten days in Montecatini: it was a refreshing time. The baths were not open for the first four days and Colonel Evans had the waters sent in a bottle to his room. Moncrieff spent the early hours of the morning and the late hours of the afternoon upon his translation of Proust. He was then on the second volume of *Le Côté de Guermantes*. He would sit at a table in a café, with two dictionaries beside him, writing by hand into an exercise book. He proceeded at an even pace, about two hundred words an hour. He worked for two hours in the morning: then we went for a long walk, before lunching off Pasta and Chianti. In London he had worked on *The Times* in some form of secretarial capacity to Northcliffe. 'I used to get paid £1,500, heavily taxed, with some expenses; here I get paid £750 untaxed but with no expenses. No,' he went on, 'it isn't hackwork, besides, what else can I do except hackwork. I haven't a creative talent. It isn't hackwork because I am enabled to enter into the mind of a writer in the way that no reader, no critic could. A writer is planning for a scene that will take place in forty pages. A special tension is created and mounts as he approaches the scene. He pictures himself writing that scene, in, shall we say, the second week in August. As I translate the book, I enter his excitement in a way that a reader cannot who reads in two hours what it took a man two months to write. No, it's not hackwork, besides I know that it's worth doing: the world will be better off for having this book on its library shelves.'

Moncrieff was a Catholic, a convert. 'I am paid by the thousand words. I am engaged in trying to interpret eternal truth in terms of such a temporal measure as two guineas a thousand words. Non-Catholics ask 'how can you get the remission of so many hours in purgatory in terms of so many penances?' There's an exact parallel I think. You need on earth a temporal yardstick to measure what cannot be measured.'

From Scott-Moncrieff, and from Eldred himself, I learnt a lot about Eldred during those ten days. Eldred was then twenty-two. He was the heir to Workington, an estate in Cumberland on the edge of Windermere. He was a member of a family that went so far back that, as a gossip columnist once said 'it made the Planta-genets seem parvenus.' He had had a curious upbringing. His mother whom he adored had died when he was eleven; his elder brother was killed in the war. That brother had been the object of all his father's ambitions. After his death his father lost interest in life. He had sent his elder son to Harrow, but was uninterested when Eldred was superannuated from Shrewsbury. When Eldred was expelled from a smaller school, he decided that the best thing to do was to give Eldred £30 a month and let him live abroad on it. When a local girl complained that as a result of Eldred's atten-tions she was pregnant he sent her a cheque for £20 and told her that he did not want to hear any more about the matter.

In the conventional sense Eldred had no education at all. He could not spell because he knew no grammar; for instance, he would spell 'didn't' 'dident' because he did not realise it was a contraction of 'did not'. He knew enough mathematics to work out his own accounts. He had never learnt any foreign languages but he spoke French, Italian, German and Spanish ungrammati-cally but colloquially and fluently, with a pleasant accent. He was an excellent mechanic, and could keep his own car in good repair. He had no interest in organised games; he had never played cricket or football. But he was a good lawn tennis player, and a keen skier. He never let himself get fat.

He never did a day's work. He considered it his job to spend an income not to earn it. He had to decide how to get the most out of whatever he received from the family estates. He never got into debt. In that he showed great character. He knew exactly what he could afford. He was glad, naturally, to be a guest, but he never cadged. A guest has to sing for his supper. All animals develop a protective covering. I wish I had known Eldred in his first years in Europe. He must have then recognised what was to be his role. He would never become a person of any consequence or position. Workington, when he inherited it, would not make him rich. He would always be on his own. He would have to fit in to other people's lives. He had to be someone whom people would like to have around. It was in his nature to become just that. He was gregarious. He was noisy. He enjoyed a good time. He was affectionate. He was an assiduous amorist. After the Second War, when he was in his middle forties, he was, when skiing, caught in a snow drift. He was completely submerged. It was great luck that the top of his ski protruding above the snow showed his companions where he was. He had lost consciousness, but during the minutes that he was being stifled, he had two substantial orgasms. It is, I believe, a medical fact that a man who is being hanged, has an orgasm as his neck breaks. A double orgasm is a proof surely of unusual potency. In his first days, when I knew him, his allowance from his father had been increased to £900 a year. A little later he broke the entail on Workington in return for an annuity of £2,000 free of tax. He could therefore manage if he was cautious; but very few young men would have been so cautious. He was resolved to be independent. He was unique. No one occupied a position in the least like his. He had a great many devoted friends. Though he was not conventionally educated, he read a great deal; invariably books of merit: he enjoyed the company of writers and of painters. He held his own in any party he attended. Parties were always more fun if he was there. At times he could cast himself for the role of jester. He would say the most outrageous things, which because he said them did not seem outrageous. He would 'camp' about the place, dancing *pas seuls* in night clubs, but he never went too far. He had an infallible sense of where to stop. He was never gross.

It was a great piece of luck for me that he came to the West Indies with me. When we started we did not know each other very well. He told me later that he had great qualms during the week before we sailed. 'You hardly know this man,' his friends had warned him. 'He's older than you are. He's got a certain position in the world. He may make social demands on you.'

I, however, had no such qualms. I was certain it would work out and I knew from earlier trips that I had made, how often I had felt the need for a companion. I had enjoyed my trip round the world, but I enjoyed this trip infinitely more. I also got more out of it as a writer, because through his technique of making friends quickly, I saw many more sides of the islands that we visited. I wrote *Hot Countries* during the trip and *Hot Countries* was the book that started me in America. Every evening he would read what I had written in the morning. His interest, his enthusiasm quickened my own interest. As I wrote in the morning I would think 'that sentence should make Eldred chuckle.'

Quite often he would make suggestions. 'Don't you think you ought to mention what the Judge of St Kitts said about that poisoning trial?' Writing is a solitary occupation. I have always been careful not to talk about my work until it is finished. Eldred was the only person to whom I have ever talked about my 'work in progress'. He would have made a good husband for a novelist. On the whole, the women novelists who have been most successful and happy in their marriages are those who have married men without professions. A woman novelist needs as much attention and cherishing in her profession as a lawyer or a politician does. She needs to have burdens taken off her shoulders, which is exactly what Eldred would have done. He would have run the home efficiently, would have kept household accounts, would have supervised her entertaining. He would have been a good lover. His annuity would have been a useful addition to the budget. His

71

wife would not have needed to write, when she was not inclined, to pay the rent. And he would have been encouraging and helpful with her work. Instead, at a later day, he linked his life with a woman of independent means who was his equivalent in many ways – a playgirl to his playboy. They made a success of their life together, but it lacked the ballast that would have been given to it by one or other having a profession.

When Eldred and I had finished our trip to the West Indies, we began to plan the next trip that we would take. We were convinced that we would take one one day, but always something intervened; he wanted to ski, I wanted to play cricket. He was constantly falling in love. And then the pattern of his life was changed by his aunt leaving him in the summer of 1930 her villa in Antibes.

It was, and is, a charming, old-fashioned house in the Chemin de l'Ermitage. It had thick walls and its garden, a narrow strip of land, ran straight down to the sea on the Garoupe side. From its wall, which had a little platform above its gate, you could see across the water the twin towers and bastions of the old town, with beyond the Baie des Anges, the long curve of the Promenade des Anglais, the villas and hotels mounting up the hill to Cimiez, and behind the snow-capped summits of the Alpes Maritimes. In one of his short stories Maupassant describes this view. He says it is one of the most beautiful in the world. I never tired of looking at it.

When his aunt told him that she was leaving it to him she said, 'Of course, I know that you will sell it sooner or later, but I'd like to think of your having some happy times here.' She believed that he was, at his age, committed to his wandering existence; but in point of fact the villa gave him the roots that he was beginning to need. It was the equivalent of a profession for him. He continued to travel. Very often he let it in the summer. Occasionally he would exchange it with me for my London flat – I spent my honeymoon there in the autumn of 1932. It became increasingly the centre of his life; without it the liaison with a companion who could not get a divorce would never have lasted from 1937 until his death in 1955.

I was to pay him many visits there, and I am still quite often the guest of the companion now married to the painter, John Strachey, to whom he left the villa. But of all those many visits, the one of which I have the warmest memories is that of the two weeks in the spring of 1931, when I worked on the manuscript of *So Lovers Dream*. It was unlike any of the other times that I spent there, because Eldred, who had recently undergone an operation for tonsilitis, was by doctor's orders 'on the wagon'. I drank wine with my meals, but to keep him company I abjured aperitifs and liqueurs. We avoided parties – not that very many were being given at that time of year – and we kept early hours. Eldred was a late riser. Breakfast was brought up to him at nine o'clock. I had had mine at eight; and usually I had written six or seven hundred words by then. Eldred's getting up was leisurely – it was almost a *levée*. He would read his paper. Before he had shaved he would go downstairs and interview his butler, a distinguished Italian who added greatly to the house's charm. He would potter about the garden, examining the rabbits and the poultry, perhaps washing down his car. By then it would be warm enough for me to write in the garden. It did not interrupt my concentration to exchange gossip as I wrote. Once when I was at work on a description of a Riviera garden, I asked him the name of a certain shrub. 'Spergum,' he answered. I did not know that he was pulling my leg. I wonder if any readers of *So Lovers Dream* were surprised to read of a garden 'scented with spergum'.

Eldred would be unlikely to reach his bathroom before ten. His bath and shaving would take an hour. I had often watched his routine in the West Indies. He proceeded at the rate of a slow motion film. Because he had no work to do, he took an hour doing what most men do in fifteen minutes. He had reddish hair, thick with a wave in it; he gave it prolonged attention. He would take the bank notes that he had scattered the previous evening on his dressing-table. He would smooth out each note, carefully removing every wrinkle, before he transferred it to his pocket book. He did not want to be dressed and ready before eleven, and he was resolved not to be. His job was to get the maximum amount of fun out of his annuity. In the same way he knew that there were only twenty-four hours in the day. They must be used to suit his whims. What was the point of getting bathed, shaved and dressed in half-an-hour, then finding himself with half-an-hour on his hands. It was too early to start reading. When he read, he liked an uninterrupted couple of hours' session.

He refused to be hurried. In the West Indies, on our arrival at Guadeloupe, we found that the launch to shore was to leave the ship half an hour earlier than we had expected. I hastened to our cabin. 'Eldred, the launch will be leaving in quarter of an hour. You'll have to get a move on.'

He shook his head. 'I can't be ready in less than half an hour.'

He had already breakfasted. He had only to shave, shower and dress. But mentally and emotionally he needed that half an hour to get himself adjusted to the day. If he did not start the day at the tempo to which he was accustomed the day was spoilt. 'If we don't get that launch, we'll have to hire one ourselves. That'll be expensive.'

'All right. I'll pay for it.'

I did not argue with him and I let him pay. Guadaloupe was our first port of call. I learnt my lesson there. He must not be hurried. It was the kind of trait that made him a very congenial companion. Selfish people usually are – by which I mean people who know their own minds and do not mean to do anything they do not want. The person who always says 'what would you like to do' can be exasperating. By the time the trip was over, I knew Eldred very well, in that and many other ways.

The country is happy that has no history and few incidents; only three in fact stand out from those two happy weeks. The first was our seeing at the local cinema of René Clair's film *Le Million*. We had heard nothing about it. We went there expecting nothing in particular. Suddenly we realised that we were watching a masterpiece: or we felt we were. We looked at each other, questioningly: was it really as funny as we were finding it? Eldred was dead sober; I had drunk only a half bottle of wine at dinner. We watched, eagerly expectant. When the struggle for the coat that contained the ticket suddenly became a football match, we lost all doubt. Yes, it was a masterpiece. We relaxed into our enjoyment.

74

Janet Kirby
Now Mrs William P. Banning

Barbara Starke

Elinor
Mrs Walcott Gibbs

Cecile

J. C. Squire's Cricket XI
Seated: Walton O'Donnell, J.C. Squire, J.B. Priestley;
Standing: R. Squire, Kenneth Lindsay, A.D. Peters, A.G. Macdonell,
J.A.R. Hockin, A.W., Squire II, E.W. Swanton, R.H. Lowe. The boy is Squire's son.

Evelyn Waugh (*centre carrying book*) flies to
Villefranche to join A.W. April 1930

A.W. with Mary. Nice, August 1931

A.W. at Villefranche. May 1931

A. W. and
Kenneth Lindsay M.P.
on a cricket tour

Barbara Starke

The manuscript of
'So Lovers Dream'

Eldred Curwen

It was for me in terms of the cinema a unique experience. Always before and always since when I have seen a film of supreme excellence, I have been prepared for it by advance publicity. It has not, as *Le Million* did, hit a virginity of sense.

During my stay at the Villa Marina, I received from Cassell's my author's copies of a collection of short stories called *Most Women*. After the title page was printed 'to Elinor Sherwin for a great many reasons'. I read that with mixed feelings.

When I had met Elinor the previous May, she had made so considerable an impression on me that, on my return to England, I had wondered whether my intentions might not become what was then called 'honourable', and three weeks before I sailed for New York I rang her up from London to give her the date of my return. The transatlantic telephone was then a novelty. It was the first time that I had used it. It was probably the first time that she had been called by it. It was a bad connection. I could hardly hear what she said. Her voice did not seem her voice. But it was dramatic all the same. And the talk did inspire her to write me a letter. The first that I had had from her. I had clearly made an impression.

I should have been wise to leave it there. But the telephone services, to whom I had complained of the bad connection, rang up to say that they were very sorry, but sometimes the static was worse than others. They were anxious that I should not be discouraged from using the transatlantic telephone; they would be happy this one time to give me a complimentary call to New York on a date and at a time of my own choosing.

It was unwise of me to accept their offer. But my Scottish instincts would not let me pass up a free transatlantic call – a very much more expensive operation then than it is now. I opted for my last night in London. I was giving a small dinner party in my flat and I confess that I felt rather grand when my housekeeper summoned me from the table to take a New York call. But it was a mistake, an anticlimax; the 'doing savoured of disrelish'. The call had been booked five days before. The atmosphere of the 'impromptu' had been lost. The first time Elinor had had no idea what was happening; she must have been excited when she was told out of the blue that London wanted her that afternoon at five; 'What on earth can this be about?' she must have thought. It was an altogether different matter to be asked on a Friday, if she could take a call on the following Wednesday at half past five. Anything during five days might turn up that she would rather do at that time. It would be a weight round her neck; an obligation in a city where people lived from day to day. It would be a nuisance. She would cease to think of me as an erratic unaccountable adventurer but a tiresome, pernickety consultant of the calendar. Moreover this time I had nothing particular to say. The first time my approach had been 'Hullo, there, why haven't I heard from you. I'm getting worried.' That call was a spontaneous outburst. The second a stereotyped reminder that I was due in New York on November 17th, a fact that she already knew – a purposeless performance; it must have cost me at least fifty per cent of the credit I had gained by the first call, and of course it turned out that the connection this time was perfect: I heard every word she said.

The second call had been typical of a frustrated courtship. I was soon to discover that Elinor was involved with a married man from whom she was not ready yet to break. The only effective role for me was a waiting one. The dedication seemed to me now as typical as the second call had been of a consistent doing of the right thing at the wrong time.

The dedication had been a gesture to myself as well as to Elinor. Three years back, on my return from Tahiti, I had written a novel *Nor Many Waters* especially for Ruth. It was published on August 15th, 1928, her birthday and Napoleon's, and I had dedicated it to her 'as a birthday present'. I wrote in a covering letter 'till I can inscribe a book to you as "my wife" I will not dedicate another of my books.' Three books of mine, including *Hot Countries*, which I would dearly have loved to dedicate to Eldred, appeared indedicate upon the market. 'The course of human events' had absolved me from that promise, but I wondered now whether there was not a fatality about dedications. I recalled that P. G. Wodehouse, in one of his dedications, had written: 'I hope that our friendship will survive this.' Looking back at my own dedications, it seemed to me that they had been not so much the cement in a friendship as the climax of one. Was that what this dedication was to prove?

Luckily this time it did not turn out that way. Elinor was to become one of my dearest friends, also one of my most important. Two years later she was to marry Wolcott Gibbs, and through her I was to meet many of my best New Yorker friends, John O'Hara, James Thurber, Charles Addams, Nathaniel Benchley, S. N. Behrman, St Clair McKelway, Geoffrey Hellman, Philip Hamberger, Hobart Weekes. It was through her indirectly that I became a member of the Coffee House, the Club where I feel most at home. No one has brought more happiness into my life than she has, but I could not foresee that, as I sat at Eldred Curwen's desk signing copies of *Most Women* and reflecting that possibly the trouble about dedications is that they are too public an endorsement at a personal relationship. The recipient is embarrassed by a public avowal of affection. 'I knew the old boy liked me, but I did not know that he did that much.' It makes him feel awkward. Is there not a parallel between the number of happy love affairs that are spoilt by marriage? I then and there made a vow never to dedicate another book. I would not run the risk of imperilling a friendship.

To that vow I have been roughly faithful. I have dedicated books to the memories of friends, and now and again to ladies once dear to me, whose lives have become divided from my own. My dedications are indeed the tombstones in a cemetery. Even the graveyard has not always brought immunity. A recent novel *A Spy in the Family* is sub-titled 'an erotic comedy', and as I was writing it I kept thinking how much it would have amused a friend who had died a few months earlier. So after the title page I wrote 'To the memory of a deeply missed friend, this indelicate story that contains no indelicate words.' One of the purposes served by a dedication is that it can give a reader an indication of the kind of book that he is being invited to read. I thought that 'indelicate story that contains no indelicate words' would give the reader precisely the warning that was needed. My surprise could not have been more complete when my publishers received from his widow through a solicitor, an indignant complaint that 'the novel though no doubt amusing, contained several descriptions of abnormal sexual activities' and that 'the dedication of such a book to her husband might be taken as implying that he was a devotee of such or similar practices.' As I agreed to have the dedication removed from the paperback edition, I thought gratefully of the number of my books that had gone out into the world indedicate. I was very glad that in the summer of 1931 I had come to that decision in Eldred Curwen's drawing-room.

I have been equally resolute in my refusal to let my friends dedicate their books to me. It was a shock, therefore, a few years back, to read my name after the title page of a fellow Tangerine's book on Port. He had not sent me a copy of it, nor had he asked my permission to dedicate it to me; a permission I should not have given. 'That's too bad' I thought. I was, and am fond of the chap. I respect his talent as a writer. 'This time I'll do my best to beat that jinx' I vowed.

But it was no good. At that time I had in Tangier a house next to his. His gardener appropriated my top soil – an unneighbourly act surely. I held him responsible, perhaps mistakenly. The coolness has been now dissolved. But I pray that no one else will ever dedicate a book to me.

The third memorable incident during my stay in the Villa Marina was the news from St John's Wood that I had been elected to MCC. I had known that I should be shortly, as I had played the last of my qualifying matches in the previous summer, and I had learnt that complimentary reports upon my play had been sent in to Lord's, but even so the official announcement did represent a genuine achievement. To-day it is relatively simple to get elected to MCC. A candidate cannot be entered under the age of fourteen, by which time it can be seen whether or not he has a natural interest in or aptitude for the game. The seating accommodation has been so enlarged that there is room for a much larger number of members; moreover the cost of the new stands has enforced the need for a larger membership. There are at the moment 15,000. My sons took less than ten years to get elected with no strings being pulled on their behalf. But in the 1920s the waiting list was very long. In those days a male could have his name entered at birth and that was what every far-seeing father did for his son. My father was not far-seeing. He never planned his life in advance. He made instantaneous decisions whenever a new issue arose. Evelyn refers to this trait in him in *A Little Learning*. He speaks of his father's 'deleterious speed'. At Oxford in spite of his love of acting, he never joined the OUDS. He thought it would be too expensive. Actually he could easily have afforded it. Later in London he joined the Savile Club instead of the Garrick. The Savile was at that time in Piccadilly where the Park Lane Hotel now stands – twenty minutes away by bus or tube from his office in Henrietta Street, Covent Garden. The Garrick on the other hand lay between his office and the tube station at Leicester Square, from which he travelled back and forth to his home in Golders Green. The Garrick would have been much more convenient; moreover, he would have found the company there more congenial as it was patronised by prominent actors and producers. At the outbreak of war he resigned from the Savile, as an economy, because he so seldom went there. He did not join another club when the war ended. Had he joined the Garrick in the first place, I do not think he would have resigned in 1914. Through not looking ahead, he deprived himself of many opportunities for conviviality.

As regards cricket, he was an enthusiastic follower of the game; he started and nourished my love of it, but he did not enter my name for MCC until 1914; this meant that my contemporaries had a sixteen-year start of me, and I could scarcely hope to be elected until I was over fifty.

During the 1920s, however, there was devised a means by which candidates with reasonable club cricket qualifications could get their election accelerated as playing members. This involved the pulling of certain preliminary strings in order to get one's name on the list of probationary candidates. Then, to justify one's presence there, one had to play in twelve trial games for MCC in which the match manager reported on one's qualities and behaviour. It took me several years even with the backing of

P. F. Warner to get on that list. Then I had to play my dozen games. It will be appreciated with what excitement, with what pride I read the announcement of my election. I could now walk into the pavilion not only for Middlesex matches – I was already a member of the county club – but for Test matches, for the Oxford and Cambridge, for the Eton and Harrow matches; I could take a guest in with me. What a pleasure to be able to take my father there. There is no comparison between the view of the play that you get when you are watching behind the bowler's arm and when you are in the members' guests enclosure, the mound or square in the grandstand. It was for this reason that in recent years my father and I had gone more often to the Oval where I was a member. But we both preferred Lord's – the centre and the home of cricket.

As a member of MCC I should be entitled to Rovers' tickets for Test matches, which would allow my friends a choice of seats in the various guests' enclosures. What a valued present that would make. I had known that I should be elected in the spring, but the tangible proof of my election warmed my heart.

I wrote to Peters and asked him to send me out an MCC scarf and tie. The red and yellow in their pristine vividness looked very garish in the Mediterranean sunlight. Eldred viewed it with disfavour. 'Never wear that,' he said 'except upon the cricket field.' He belonged to a generation that held it to be bad form to wear an old Etonian or a Brigade tie except when you were visiting your old school or attending a reunion dinner. I could see his point. I never thought it good form for debutantes who had been presented at Court to go on to supper at the Ritz with their feathers in their hair, or for men on their way back from Ascot to wear in their button-holes a Royal Enclosure badge. It was as though the wearers of these insignia were saying 'I may be supping in the same restaurant as you, or walking down the same stretch of pavement, but I am, you will observe, a person belonging to a superior world.'

MCC took a different view of its red and yellow. In the following summer, needing a new blazer, I ordered an MCC one. I was soon made to realise that I had committed a gross solecism and the captain of the side, not in private, but before the other members, warned me that I should cause grave offence to certain veterans who had worn Marylebone blazers in the days of W. G. Grace.

'The old school tie' is the subject of much genial satire. I have been told that the MCC colours came into disrepute because any man whose name was entered at birth could become a member without being a cricketer; and that real cricketers did not like to see 'rabbits' wearing the same colours as themselves. A man of seventy-five wearing a faded MCC blazer could suggest that he had been a member half a century before, in the homeric days of the great doctor.

This snobbery of colours would have made an amusing essay for Max Beerbohm. In the 1930s there was a cartoon in *Punch* by Fougasse, showing an athlete in various forms of sartorial array. 'If you are playing for the old Crundonians' the caption ran, 'you may wear a Forester scarf, an Incog blazer, an IZ sweater, a Nondescript belt, but the one thing you must not wear is anything Old Crundonian.'

A few years ago in the University match at Lord's, a number of Oxonians went in to bat wearing club and county caps. They were vigorously reproved in *The Daily Telegraph* by E. W. Swanton.

At any rate I did not wear my MCC blazer again upon the cricket field. I took it around with me on cruises and on beaches: in the Riviera and the Caribbean. It was a familiar sight in St Thomas in the 1950s when it was surmounted by a wide-brimmed cha-cha hat. I used it as a writing coat, and several press interviews recorded my wearing of it at my desk in the Algonquin. Finally it fell to pieces in the Macdowell Colony in the early 60s. It embarrassed me on the cricket field, but it was a good friend, the companion of many contented hours.

VII

After two weeks at the Villa Marina, since Eldred was expecting a cousin from England I had to look for a new perch. With the Welcome closed, I decided on the Colombe d'Or at St Paul de-Vence. Of all the lovely villages crowding that lovely coast, I question if there is any lovelier. High on a hill, it is complete and self-contained. The same walls that guarded it against Saracen invasions surround it still. The ground falls down sharply on every side. There is no development outside its walls. There it stands with its bastions, its tower and its spire, unchanged through the centuries. Two roads lead past it on the way to Vence. Either way you look at it across the valley it seems 'to breathe the enchantment of the Middle Ages.'

Nor does it deceive you once you have passed through its gateway. There are the narrow streets, the courtyard with the fountain; antique shops and galleries, more now than there were then. You can walk right round it along the walls in twenty minutes. The southern tip is pointed like the prow of a ship. Below it is a cemetery.

I have several times used it in a magazine short story. The hero drives the heroine out from Nice. He lunches her amply on a shaded terrace, then after their coffee, he takes her for a slow stroll round the town. They stand in the pointed apex of the walls. The valleys stretch towards the sea. It is as superb a panorama as the coast has for offering. The cemetery lies below them. He points it out to her. His other arm goes round her shoulders. 'We're a long time dead,' he says.

It was always at the Colombe d'Or that my hero lunched her; a world renowned restaurant-hotel, housing a fine collection of modern paintings, that lies just outside the walls. Its garden is lined with orange trees, and the square courtyard set with tables. How pleasant it would be, I thought, to sit there after breakfast at work upon a manuscript; and so it was, but I had not recognised

the difference between the Colombe d'Or as a two-star restaurant
to which you drove out from Nice or Antibes, to an excellent and
expensive lunch or dinner, and the Colombe d'Or as a hotel where
you lived en pension at 60 Francs a day – the Franc was then at
120 to the pound. In the first place, breakfast was the only meal
which a *pensionnaire* was allowed to take on the terrace. For
lunch and dinner he had to eat indoors. The menus which he was
offered though ample and adequate were inevitably very different
from those with which visitors were being regaled. That you
would expect. But it was a little tantalising after you had finished
your table d'Hôte meal, served promptly at 7.30 p.m., to watch
flaming chafing dishes and high crested soufflés being wheeled
past you to the terrace. There was no lounge or hall where you
could sit and read, out of sight of these self-indulgent revellers.
If you wanted to avoid them, you had to go outside and there was
nowhere to go except one of the small dark bars inside the walls.
There was no sidewalk café where you could loiter over a coffee
and a *fine* and watch life go by. In a small dark bar you tend to
finish your *fine* quickly and order a second. After two *fines* you
are not quite fresh for work next day. I preferred to stay on the
hard seat where I had dined, with my book on the table, between
my elbows, my head supported on my hands until my eyelids
began to close.

There were other disadvantages. I did not have a car. There
were three or four buses running into Nice but that required a
half-day excursion. It was not worth going in unless one stayed
for lunch – which cut into the day's work, besides involving me
in the cost of missing a lunch that had been paid for. There was
no swimming. Nor was there anywhere to walk, except down a
very steep hill which meant a strenuous climb back. When I am
working, I like to take long walks along the level – the Promenade
des Anglaise is ideal – thinking out my stories. In fact I did not
have nearly enough exercise. Moreover I was lonely. I lacked
company. I had no friends. There was no equivalent for the
Garden Bar, nor for the acquaintances that I had made in villas.
Gwen Le Gallienne, the painter – whose father Richard had
been a good friend of my father's – had a studio in the ramparts.

Sometimes she used to come to the Colombe d'Or for breakfast and we would gossip over her morning cigarette. But she led a very self-contained industrious existence. She avoided bars. The most congenial routine usually contains, somewhere or other, in the course of the day, two hours that are a little difficult to live through. But at St Paul the only really good part of the day was the morning until eleven o'clock when I sat on the terrace, writing, looking out over the valley, with the pigeons fluttering along the wall. At eleven, the preparations for lunch began, and I had to change my table for the one at which I would eat my own lunch later. By the end of the third day I came to realise that I should have to get away. I was unboundedly relieved when I learnt that the Welcome had reopened its bedrooms though not its restaurant. Nothing could have suited me better. To sleep at the Welcome; to wake with the reflections of the water flickering on the ceiling and not to be obligated to eat two pension meals a day.

I seldom go to the South of France without visiting St Paul and lunching at the Colombe d'Or. My enjoyment of the excellent meal there is heightened by the knowledge that I shall be driving back into Nice in three hours time. St Paul is a 'must' for every tourist, but for me in 1931 it was a prison.

Shortly after my return to Villefranche, I received a letter addressed by hand with a St Jean-Cap Ferrat postmark. It was from the Villa Mauresque. It was signed W. S. Maugham. The writer asked if I would care to come out to lunch on a choice of days in the following week. It enquired if I played tennis. I had only met Maugham once: in 1922 and very briefly at a lunch organised by Arnold Lunn for the contributors to the anthology that he had edited, *Georgian Stories*. We had scarcely exchanged a word, and I did not believe that W.S.M. would have remembered it. But I had met, when I was staying with Eldred Curwen, a young man who had told me that he was lunching with Maugham the following Friday. I told him how much I admired Maugham and how much I would like to meet him. That was, I presumed, the reason for the invitation.

I was flattered and excited. My apprenticeship as a novelist was influenced and coloured by four writers: Compton Mackenzie was the first. While I was writing *The Loom of Youth* I took a week off at the end of the second part, and re-read *Sinister Street*, vol. 2. This had a marked effect on the style of the second half. In a prisoner of war camp, in Mainz, I was introduced by Hugh Kingsmill to George Moore's reminiscences, *Memoirs of my Dead Life* and *Hail and Farewell*. Under their influence I wrote a book of memoirs called *Myself when Young*, and made an attempt at short stories told in the first person. In 1922 I read *The Forsyte Saga*. I learnt from it how to weave a number of characters and lives into a continuous narrative by starting each chapter with a different character as the protagonist. Then in 1925 on a visit to G. B. Stern's villa in Diano Marina I re-read the *The Trembling of a Leaf* and *The Moon and Sixpence*. That spring *The Painted Veil* came out.

I have seldom read a novel with more excitement. I was staying at the Savile Club; the book was among those that were on loan from Harrod's circulating library. I hurried back from dinner parties so that I could go on reading it, and lest another member should take it up to bed with him, I concealed it behind the *Encyclopaedia Britannica*. Maugham not only influenced my style of writing, but my ideas and feelings about myself. When I was staying with G. B. Stern, her husband Geoffrey Holdsworth and I had discussed the possibilities of an escape to the South Sea Islands where living was cheap and dusky damsels were accessible. He was married, whereas I was not, so the problem was simpler for me. I fancy that G. B. Stern was afraid that the story of Gauguin might have a dangerous effect on her husband. *The Constant Nymph*, which had been published the previous autumn, had also made her apprehensive.

I was in Diano Marina in April. During the previous winter I had written a novel entitled *Kept*. The central character, a kept woman, was made symbolic of post-war London. I made the *raisonneur* reflect

. . . well and weren't we all kept really. The whole lot of us one way and another? Weren't we living all of us in the reflection of a past quality, on the strength of something that had been done for us. There was Vernon Archer, living on his reputation selling because once he had been inspired indifferent work; there was Manon Granta wedded to wealth, because eight generations back some sire of hers had earned a monarch's favour; with Heritage kept by the industry of a grandfather; and himself for one half-hour's act of courage, entitled for the rest of his life to maintenance and promotion and respect. They were of a piece really with that poor creature selling matches. He, too, was being kept by what little remained of public gratitude for the men who had stood firm at Mons. Kept, all of them, in their different way.

The book did rather well, not only in England but in the USA. It was, indeed, the first of my books to evoke any interest there. My stock on the literary bourse went up. The two novels that I had published since my first, *The Loom of Youth*, had not been received with any interest. They had not deserved to be. They were presented as contemporary novels but they were not dated. The war was an obstacle. If you wanted to write a story that covered a number of years, and were going to place it before the war, the reader would say to himself, 'This is happening in 1910. In four years time the convulsion of war will have altered the pattern of every individual life. No matter what the confusion into which the characters have got themselves by June 1914, in six weeks they will have a way out of their problems.' The writer had in the war an obvious *deus ex machina*. And because he had, the reader could not take a complete interest in the fates of characters whose fates would not be worked out in terms of a logical process of cause and effect. If, on the other hand the author were to place the beginning of his story in 1919, a ten years' development would land the narrative in a period that was not yet history. No one knew in 1919 what the world would be like in 1930. Would there be a revolution? There were rumblings below the surface. How many European thrones had not collapsed in the last five years? Might not scientists in their laboratories have achieved discoveries that would alter the condition of mankind? Might not the atom be split? Unless a novel was definitely prophetic, like *Brave New World*, there was an atmosphere of unreality about it. The only alternative was to place the novel in no particular time. But this is unsatisfactory, too. If you do not know when a sequence of actions is taking place, you do not know to whom it is taking place. Are these post-war or pre-war characters? That was the problem in 1922, but by 1925 everything was easier. The narrator had a space of six years to move in: a post-war character could be an adult. Moreover I had learnt from Galsworthy how to confine the actions and development of a number of characters within the radius of a single summer. *Kept* was topical; and it told a dramatic story. Critics and readers began to feel that I was not, after all, a one-book writer. Editors took a new interest in me. I started to sell short stories to the 'glossy' magazines. The *Daily Mirror* commissioned me to write a serial. My income trebled. I was twenty-seven and the auguries were good, but I was at war within myself. An inner voice was whispering that I was limiting myself and my potentialities as a writer by letting myself be caught up in a succession of London parties. There was a world elsewhere; a fuller, more dramatic world. Moreover I was tempted by the prospect of those dusky damsels by the palm-fringed beaches of Polynesia and the brown rivers of Malaysia. To my friends it seemed that the ball lay at my feet, but I was without the urge to kick it. In the summer of 1926 I resigned my half-time post as literary adviser to Chapman and Hall, and booked myself a round-the-world ticket, with the Messageries Maritimes. It would be hard for a writer to be more influenced by another than I was by Maugham. I was very excited at the prospect of a visit to the Villa Mauresque.

It was not a party: only Gerald Haxton, Maugham's secretary and travelling companion, was there. As it was to turn out, that first meeting was typical of most of our future ones. Usually they were *à trois*; With Gerald Haxton before the war and with Alan Searle afterwards. I fancy that under those conditions I saw him at his best, at his most relaxed. My book *My Brother Evelyn and other portraits* contains a long essay upon Maugham. Many people have told me that they felt ill at ease with him. I never did, indeed I had to resist a temptation to be over-confidential. He was, I always felt, the one person in the world who would understand whatever particular problem I might have. He would diagnose the symptoms, as a doctor would, and if there was a remedy he would suggest it. But I never did confide in him. Possibly because I knew what he would say. 'If that's your trouble, then you must learn to live with it.' Which is the answer for most of our emotional ailments, after we are thirty.

Maugham was at this time fifty-seven, active and healthy, playing golf or tennis every day. He was temperate; he never drank too much. He was too dignified to lose his self-control. Moreover, he wanted to be at his desk with a clear mind next morning. At this period he had himself served after dinner a pleasant potion that tasted like a rum punch, but which, in fact, contained no alcohol. I suspect that what he enjoyed most was his dry martini before lunch. In *The Fall of Edward Barnard* – his story about the South Seas that more than any other acted on me as a magnet – he made one of his characters, who had served a gaol sentence for fraud, remark: 'When I had nothing better to do in the penitentiary I used to amuse myself by thinking out new cocktails, but when you come down to brass tacks, there's nothing to beat a Dry Martini.' I wish he could have come to Tangier during his last few years so that I could have shown him one of Porte's martinis which are served in a hock glass with a sliver of lemon peel curved round the inside of the rim.

Writers, Maugham has often said, have their ups and downs. But there were no downs in his career, not during his last fifty years, after the success of his play *Lady Frederick* in 1907, until at the very end came the slow downward curve of the parabola as he reached retirement.

In 1931 his reputation was at its peak. He had made his reputation as a dramatist, and though during the '20s he continued to enjoy a series of stage successes – *East of Suez, Our Betters* (written in 1915), *The Letter, The Constant Wife* – *Of Human Bondage* was being followed by a series of superb novels and collections of stories: *The Moon and Sixpence, The Trembling of a Leaf, The Painted Veil, The Casuarina Tree,* then in 1930 the hilarious *Cakes and Ale* which set the literary world chuckling in a way that no other book has done during my lifetime. He was the most discussed writer of the day. He was also the object of a great deal of curiosity and conjecture. He was little seen in London. He had been a familiar Mayfair figure before the war. As Robin Maugham has explained in *Somerset and all the Maughams,* it was impossible for Gerald Haxton to come to England, so that if, with his marriage broken, Maugham were to have a base, it had to be outside England. He began the reconstruction of the Villa Mauresque in 1927. His *A Personal Record* gives an account of the changes that he made to it. It was to become a very lovely house, with gardens, terraces, a swimming pool. On its walls was a collection of modern paintings that was to fetch no small part of a fortune at Sotheby's in the 1960s. Rumours of the house's lavish opulence were to be part of London's gossip. No English writer had ever made so much money. He became an object of legend, of a slightly sinister legend because of his association with Gerald Haxton.

That legend was quickened by the frequent oblique references that he made to himself in *Cakes and Ale* and in his short stories, many of which were told in the first person. Readers felt they already knew him by his books, to an extent that rarely happens to a writer. One would not get much insight into Arnold Bennett's personal idiosyncrasies from *The Old Wives' Tale,* nor of Joseph Conrad's from *Victory.* Readers felt they knew Maugham so well from his books that they were a little disconcerted to find that he was not as like his own picture of himself as they had expected.

I was on my guard when I met him, knowing his books almost by heart. The 'I' of his stories could be often very snubbing. In '*The Pool*' an expatriate Scotsman talking nostalgically of London, says: 'And I like the Strand too. What are those lines about God and Charing Cross?' The 'I' of the narrative quotes them, the expatriate gives a faint sigh. 'I've read "The Hound of Heaven". It's a bit of all right.' 'It's generally thought so,' I murmured. What a drenching of cold water.

I knew that he did not like to be spoken to about his books. I had read *Ashenden* more than once. In the story 'His Excellency' he makes Ashenden, his *alter ego*, say of the Ambassador with whom he was dining, 'He mentioned in passing a character in one of Ashenden's novels, but did not make any other reference to the fact that his guest was a writer. Ashenden admired his urbanity. He disliked people to talk to him of his books in which indeed once written he took small interest and it made him self-conscious to be praised or blamed to his face. Sir Herbert Wither-spoon flattered his self-esteem by showing that he had read him, but spared his delicacy by withholding his opinion of what he had read.'

I went to the Villa Mauresque resolved that I would not mention any of his books. But I felt so much at my ease that I could not resist asking him if he considered *Of Human Bondage* his best book. 'I haven't read it since I corrected the last proofs. I wouldn't know.' Afterwards, thinking over the lunch, I wondered whether I should have put that question. I never felt self-conscious when I was with him, but afterwards I would put myself in the confessional. 'Should I have said that? Was I *gauche* at that point? Did I miss an opportunity of making a quick repartee?' And that is a form of masochism to which I do not normally expose myself.

For the most part we talked about the far countries that we had both visited. Siam, the F.M.S. and the South Seas, Tahiti in particular. I had met one or two of the people that he had. It did not seem to me to be as changed as might have been expected. I mentioned that in *Cakes and Ale* he had referred to my brother having said in the *Evening Standard* that it was a mistake to write novels in the first person. Evelyn, I said, had written no such article. He shrugged. I asked him if he had met my brother. 'Yes and No', he said. 'I met him when I was with Godfrey Winn· Godfrey introduced him to me, but not me to him; paying me the compliment of assuming that he would know who I was. Apparently your brother didn't.'

I had the good sense not to suggest that my brother may have been perfectly aware whom he was meeting.

I cannot remember what we ate or drank. Alfred Kazin, in a

long account of his post-war visits to the Villa Mauresque, states that his host was at particular pains about the menus that his chef served. I was not aware of this. Perhaps he did not exert himself particularly on my account. I recall the excellence of the small canapés – usually egg and anchovy – that accompanied the pre-lunch dry martini; after the war I remember an Avocado fool of which he was proud; he had, he said, the only Avocado tree in the Riviera. I did not dine there very often but when I did I was invariably served an excellent champagne. The lunch that I was given by Alan Searle in 1969 in Monte Carlo, with a vintage Krug as an aperitif, a Montrachet with the fish and Chateau Ausone with the entrée was infinitely superior to anything I ever tasted at the Villa Mauresque.

VII

For me in Villefranche it was a warm beneficent summer. It was
hard to believe that anyone else had any troubles. My only real
worry was my father's health. As I have already said, he had had a
bad winter, he was not well when I had been in England, and in
the appalling weather that followed Easter, his general condition
deteriorated. He felt sick and giddy, with lights dancing before his
eyes. In the last letter that he wrote me, five days before his
death, he said, 'I feel very like the dyspepsia I got in 1931 before
we went to Villefranche, but I have never felt anything like as
as bad as I did then.'

I think that he had been over-working. Retirement is a difficult experience. He had always driven himself hard, and he could
not suspend the pressure all at once. During the early part of
1930 he wrote Chapman and Hall's Centenary volume, *A
Hundred Years of Publishing*. It is not a book that could hope to
have a large sale, but it has a genuine reference value: it is
admirably composed. The sections about Dickens are written with
warmth and wit, and John Farrar has told me that he very often
concluded his lectures on the publisher's role by quoting the last
paragraph which presents the publisher seated at the end of the
day surrounded by the books that bear his imprint. It is a full
length book, and the writing of it took a lot out of him. No
sooner was that book finished than he started the rewriting and
completion of his autobiography which he had started in 1919
and put away. He was also doing an occasional article or review for
the *Spectator* or *Fortnightly Review*. In addition he was reading
and reporting on all the manuscripts that were offered to Chapman and Hall. He was very punctilious about these reports.
When I had been a reader, working in the same office as my
father, I had contented myself with noting N.B.G. against manuscripts that seemed impossible, and on those that seemed promising I would merely write, 'A novel about the conflict of the

generations in an upper middle class English family. An echo of Galsworthy but dramatically told; I think it is worth your looking at.' Then at the end of the week we would discuss it along with other manuscripts. My father wrote actual criticisms of half the manuscripts that came in, two to three hundred words on each. It seemed to me a great waste of time. But he enjoyed it, in a way. He wrote his reports wittily, and he appreciated the chuckle that went round the table when he read it out at the Board meeting on Friday. He liked the proof of his work that was provided by the pile of his reports. There was something to show for the hours that he had spent at his desk. There was also a trace of masochism in his need to present himself as a 'driven man'. Evelyn stressed this point in his character sketch of him in *A Little Learning*. I had overlooked it, perhaps because I was closer to him in sympathy and was less aware of traits that might cause irritation. Evelyn reminds the reader of the extent to which my father was a born actor, who was constantly casting himself in different roles. One of these was the 'driven man'. He would throw the back of his hand against his forehead. 'I'm so driven,' he would exclaim. When he was not driven, he drove himself.

During his first fifteen months of retirement, he worked harder than he had when he went each morning to his desk in Henrietta Street. Moreover he worked alone upstairs, in the room that had once been our nursery; it was warmer than his own library downstairs, but he did not like being alone. He missed the constant dramatic interruptions of an office; the official mail, the telephone calls, the visits from authors and agents; the various problems brought to him by the staff that was under his control. It imposed all of it a strain on him, but it stimulated him. Within three or four years of his retirement he had built up for himself with acquaintances and neighbours a routine that was filled with an hour to hour eventfulness. People were always dropping in to see him. He moved to Highgate where there was a more congenial social life. There was the Highgate Institute which had a collection of magazines and newspapers, and acted as a club. His diary was full of engagements, but that was in the future. In 1930 and 1931 he was between two worlds, and had not got adjusted to the new one. He was lonely, and in consequence overworked himself. He was never to work so hard again; in fact he gave up active writing; he had said all he had to say and contented himself with occasional reviews and essays. He was never to feel really ill again until the very end.

I think I found the right cure for his complaint when I suggested that he should come out to Villefranche in the early summer. He needed sunlight and a change of atmosphere. He loved France dearly, but he had never been further south than Avignon. The Riviera would open a new world for him.

His illness was not improved by Evelyn's being ill at the same time. Evelyn had gone to spend a few days at The Beetle and Wedge, a riverside hotel that is mentioned in H. G. Wells' *Mr. Polly*, and that was now owned by Philip Saintsbury – a charming member of the Meynell clan, a bright figure of the '20s whose star set too soon. Evelyn returned unexpectedly on the 29th of April, with a temperature of 101. Something was wrong with his mouth, he said. He would have to have all his teeth out. Two days later, his throat came out in ulcers. A hospital nurse was sent for. The family doctor did not know what was wrong. It eventually transpired that he had eaten some poisoned watercress at the Beetle and Wedge. There ensued at 145 North End Road, a comedy of which my brother at least saw the humour. It was, he said, *les malades jalouses*. My father wanted to have all the attention, always: particularly from his wife, particularly when he was ill. Evelyn was not a good patient; he took a violent dislike to his nurse. Her presence irritated him. She had the good sense to realise this and sat outside the room on a chair, reading. The house was not centrally warmed, and she wrapped herself in a dressing gown. For five days between May 2 and May 7 there are practically no entries in my father's diary – the only time when there were no entries until the last days of his life.

In a mood of contrition which was not rare with him, Evelyn ordered from his wine merchant a dozen quarter bottles of Perrier-douet. My father enjoyed them but found them liverish. By May 11, life had returned to normal; Evelyn's trench mouth was cured, and my parents had decided to take a week's holiday in

Sussex. Evelyn celebrated their joint recovery with a gift to my father of £5 on the condition that the sum was spent in its entirety within a week. But a week in Sussex would not, he knew, be sufficient, particularly as the weather was very bad, Patsy Henderen's benefit match at Lord's on the Whitsuntide weekend being completely ruined by the rain. He now decided that he must make the experiment of a four week visit to the South of France and on Friday the 29th of May he and my mother started on the most ambitious excursion of their lives.

They took it in easy stages. They crossed by the Newhaven and Dieppe boat, spending the night in Paris; on the following day they caught a train which reached Marseilles at 10.45 P.M. I met them there. I had booked rooms for them in the Terminus Hotel. Next day we caught a morning train that reached Villefranche soon after three o'clock. I provided from the buffet a picnic of ham sandwiches. My parents' summer holidays had been usually spent in the north of France, St Malo, Avranches, Caudebec-en-Caux or further north in Flanders, Bruges especially; once they had taken a cruise through the Norwegian Fjords. They had never seen 'the palms, the sunlight, and the South'. It was exciting to see the excitement on their faces after we had passed St Raphael, and reached the red rocks round Agay; an excitement that mounted after we passed La Napoule, and indeed is there anywhere in the world a lovelier stretch of coastline?

It was a very, very happy holiday. Villefranche was the ideal place for a couple of my parents' age. It was easy for them to take excursions of an unexacting nature. The morning climb to the Octroi to catch the trolley into Nice was the only real demand upon their energy. Everything else involved a stroll along the level. There was in Villefranche itself the twenty minutes walk to the Darse. In Nice there was the Jardin d'Albert Ier. Sometimes they would take a *fiacre* along the Promenade des Anglais, and sip a coffee in the Café de la Méditerranée. Often they would lunch at Mont Boron, in a restaurant that no longer exists with a terrace looking out over the bay. Quite often my parents lunched alone, leaving me to remain on the harbour with my manuscript. It was the first time that they had been on a holiday when they had not been forced to have all their meals en pension at the same hotel. They appreciated the variety that they could thus enjoy. We took a number of excursions. Once we went to the Casino at Cannes so that I could get the material for a description of it in my novel. My mother and I went on a bus trip to Gourdon and to Grasse where we saw the perfume factories. We lunched the three of us at the Columbe d'Or – lunch at that time, I am reminded by my father's diary, was thirty francs a head. Then, the franc was 120 to the pound. A film was being made there at the time. This was a cause of great excitement to my father. Eighteen months later I was to see the film. The shots at the Colombe d'Or occupied a bare three minutes. It was very much a B film, in French, but it added immeasurably to my father's enjoyment of the day; Gwen Le Gallienne happened to be lunching there. That too was a treat for my father.

In those days the large Customs shed did not exist at Villefranche. I cannot with my mind's eye picture it all as it was then. I fancy that the sea ran up close to the path that runs above the parking place towards the Darse. Boule was played there, certainly; and we used to bathe off the rocks. That short walk from the hotel to the ramparts of Vauban's fortress was my father's favourite. He used to walk there after breakfast smoking his first pipe of the day. *Il fume toujours son pipe, votre père,* Cécile said to me. It was a warm summer, but my father always wrapped a scarf round his neck. He also wore the same tweed suit that he wore in England in the summer. It had a waistcoat, and he also wore a light-weight vest and long-legged under-pants. 'I like to feel wool against my skin,' he said. He did not seem stifled. Yet in London he would be wearing precisely the same clothes when I would be wrapped in a great coat. And he would insist on opening windows even on winter nights. He enjoyed a bracing atmosphere. He liked to feel the wind on his face, but because of his asthma, he wanted to protect his chest. I often remember this contrast when I see how heavily the Moroccans wrap themselves on the hottest July afternoon. Yet they never seem overhot in their brown rough djelabas. Perhaps they – and my father – have reason on their side.

My father had brought out with him the proofs of his auto-biography *One Man's Road*. There was half a chapter still to write. He wrote it on his second day. I can still see him coming to where I was sitting over my manuscript, with a broad grin on his face. 'It's finished,' he said. It was not only a book that was finished, but his writing life. He was to write little more, but as I said in my chapter on him in *My Brother Evelyn*, the last decade of his life was to prove in a great many ways, the happiest.

I had read a good deal of his autobiography already. But it was at Villefranche that I read it through, for the first time from start to finish. Naturally I was absorbed by it. In the early 50s I suggested that Chapman and Hall should reissue it, with a preface by myself, but the idea did not receive much encouragement. Evelyn suggested that I should prepare a miscellany of our father's writings, that would include extracts from *One Man's Road*, from his Newdicate Prize Poem and the poem he wrote on the death of his brother Alick and that was privately printed. My father had also written a collection of poems 'Legends of the Wheel', in the days of the cycling boom. Some of these might be worth reprinting. There should also be examples of his correspondence. Some of his very best writing went into his letters. Many of his friends kept the letters that he had written them all their lives. Only a few years ago I received a collection of letters that he had written to the Parish priest at St Augustine's Kilburn, some at the start of the century, others in the 30s – annual letters in reply to birthday congratulations. They were wonderfully vivid and alive. They are now in the library of the University of Texas. He used to hope that one day a selection of his letters would be issued. But the difficulty of such a project was that his best letters were written to people of whom the public had never heard, and the witty references to mutual friends would not be understood. Elaborate editing and the writing of innumerable footnotes would be required. For me living nine months of the year abroad, it was a task beyond my powers. I suggest it as an act of *pietas* to my nephew Auberon or my niece Harriet.

Very likely Evelyn was right about *One Man's Road*, and it has only a reference value now. Certainly the first part is much the best. In autobiographies it invariably is. A man has usually by the time he is thirty, chosen, or had chosen for him, the path that his career will follow. Nothing unexpected is likely to happen to him. Tolstoi said of Karenin – then in his thirties – that he had ceased to be interesting, because one knew what to expect for him, from him. He would rise in his career. Fresh laurels waited him. But he had ceased to be potential. For some men in public life the concluding decades are of dramatic content because they are concerned with big events, but in themselves the authors of such autobiographies act as reporters, as *raisonneurs*. It is very rare that they are themselves the creators and controllers of big events; for them to be that, they have to be Bismarcks, de Gaulles, Winston Churchills.

It has been said that every man has one book in him, and every man's life is of interest up till the point when he has decided on and made a start in his career, and until he has found the woman with whom he is going to share that life. Up till that point he is at the mercy of the winds of chance. Most young men in their first year at a University have four or five roads open to them. It is luck which one they choose. But the choice once made, there is an absence of the unexpected and that is what makes or mars a narrative, the wondering as to what is going to happen next.

There is another reason why the first half of an autobiography is more interesting – certainly why *One Man's Road* is. In the first part the author is dealing with characters who are either no longer alive or no longer an active part of the author's life – schoolmasters come into this category. It is not easy, it is very often impossible to write honestly of business associates with whom one is brought into daily contact. My father could write honestly of his first employer, Wolcott Balestier, Kipling's brother-in-law; he could write of W. L. Courtney, his tutor at Oxford, who had introduced him to Chapman and Hall and had resigned from the Board in 1925; he could also write of his cousin Edmund Gosse, who had introduced him to the world of letters and who had died in 1929; but he could not write honestly of his current problems with his co-directors at Chapman and Hall. He had to pretend that he was happy with them, which he was very far from being. Nor could he write with complete honesty about his sons. He did not write about the troubles that I had had at school, troubles that led to the headmaster asking my father to take me away from school at the end of a term that need not necessarily have been my last; troubles that I described in my own autobiography. He could not refer to my first marriage. This meant that he had to present a very incomplete picture of his life between the years 1914 and 1922. My wife Barbara was the daughter of an old friend, W. W. Jacobs. When I was with the B.E.F. in France, and later when I was a prisoner of war in Germany she stayed at Underhill going each morning into London to take classes first at Queen's and then at Bedford College. She and Evelyn became close friends, as he has described in *A Little Learning*; they decorated the old nursery with modern cubist frescoes. When Barbara and I married in July 1919, we made our home at Underhill, making a study drawing-room in the old nursery. Although a year later, we built a bunga-low under the downs in Sussex, Underhill remained our base. The two families were very close, with constant exchange of visits, with Barbara's brothers and sisters regarding Underhill as a home; Evelyn was at home, too in the Jacobs' house at Berkhamstead. The break-up of the marriage in January 1922 must not only have been a great blow to my father, but it meant the cutting of innumerable links. It would not have been possible for him to write a completely true story of the war and the immediate post-war years without mentioning Barbara.

His treatment of Evelyn in the book must seem to the modern reader extra-ordinary. Evelyn published *Decline and Fall* in 1928, and *Vile Bodies* in January 1930. He was immediately recognised as one of the most significant of the younger writers. Yet in his father's autobiography published in September 1931 there is no reference to him as a writer. There are some charming and warm descriptions of his boyhood, but after stating that he won the senior history scholarship at Hertford College, Oxford, in December 1921, there is no reference to him of any kind. There are a few pages about post-war Oxford, but no picture of Evelyn in Oxford, nor of the many friends he made there, many of whom became my father's friends.

Readers of *A Little Learning* will understand how this came about. Evelyn did not have the Oxford career for which his father had hoped. He took a bad third, his scholarship was taken away, and he left Oxford without a degree. That was in July 1924. During the next three and a half years he led an existence that in *A Little Learning* is the chapter headed as 'in which our hero's fortunes fall very low'. *A Little Learning* ends in 1925. During the next two years they were to fall lower. He went as a schoolmaster from one establishment to another, invariably to one lower in the social order. It was not conducive to my father's peace of mind. Evelyn was to write of this period, 'In early manhood, for a short time, I was the cause of anxiety that bordered on despair.' Most of this time he was making Underhill his base; he added in a later chapter, 'the intermittent but frequent presence of a dissipated and not always respectful spendthrift disturbed the tranquility of the home to which he always looked for refuge.'

Evelyn gave little sign of adopting literature as a career. In the summer of 1927 he was taken on the staff of the *Daily Express* on probation, and given a three months' contract on a low salary. At the end of the three months the *Daily Express* (if it had retained his services, it would have had to pay him an official salary) terminated this agreement. London newspapers at this time frequently made such arrangements with young men down from the Universities. They got the services of an intelligent and presumably ambitious young man for a small cost, and there was the chance that they might find a promising journalist. They did not detect such promise in Evelyn. They did not print a line he wrote; but fifteen months later the man who had fired him, was paying the author of *Decline and Fall* thirty guineas a thousand words.

Evelyn had been commissioned by Tom Balston of Duckworth to write a book on Rosetti, and been paid an advance of £50. This was another cause of worry for my father. He himself never paid an author money until the MSS. was delivered. He was afraid that Evelyn would never write the book and that he himself would be responsible for the return of the £50. I have told the story of these years in my chapter on Evelyn in my collection of autobiographical portraits. They were a great strain upon my father. Then suddenly the pressure was released. In January 1928, Evelyn became engaged to Evelyn Gardner. To finance this project he went into the country and wrote a novel. That novel was *Decline and Fall*. Two months before it was published, the two Evelyns were married surreptitiously. It seemed that my father had a delightful last chapter for his book. But in the summer of 1929 Evelyn's wife ran off with another man. In the following year Evelyn was admitted to the Roman Catholic communion. That whole story in the spring of 1931 when my father was at work on *One Man's Road* was too close for its emotion to be recollected in tranquility. Better not to attempt it. The most surprising feature of this omission is that it did not at the time seem extraordinary that Evelyn Waugh's father should publish an autobiography that did not mention the fact that his younger son was the day's most dominant young novelist. In his *A Hundred Years of Publishing* he paid a warm tribute to Evelyn's excellence. He had no doubt about the quality of his son's writing. But the fact that he makes no mention of Evelyn's early manhood, makes his portrait of himself very incomplete.

His book has proved a warning to me. My autobiography ended in the summer of 1930. This present narrative is confined to the year 1931. I do not intend ever to write a consecutive narrative about the new life that began with my marriage in October 1932.

During his marriage, Evelyn had a flat in Islington, in Cannonbury Square. He abandoned it when his marriage broke and again he made his base in his parents' house. He kept his clothes there, and such few personal possessions as he retained. He did not want a flat of his own. He found it easier to borrow one from a friend, when he was in London; quite often he borrowed mine. In my mother's diary there is a note against May 27, two days before their departure for Villefranche 'Evelyn returns'. Maybe he stayed on at Underhill; at any rate on June 4 a letter posted in Paris announced that he was planning to 'join us shortly'. He arrived on June 9 accompanied by Patrick Balfour (now Lord Kinross), Keith Winter, and a young painter who for reasons that will soon become obvious I would prefer not to name.

I had only met Patrick once before and then very briefly after the theatre in Beatrice Lillie's dressing-room. I had been struck by his elegance, good looks and easy manners, but I was on my guard with him. He was Mr Gossip of the *Daily Sketch*, and one of the models for the Earl of Balcains in *Vile Bodies*. I was not sure if I should like him. Gossip writers had a dubious reputation in the days of 'The Bright Young People'. Hostesses wanted their parties to be 'written up'. They were indignant when gossip writers accorded less attention to them than they did to other hostesses; they pretended to be annoyed when their privacy was not respected. In consequence, in self defence, gossip writers tended to be supercilious and arrogant. I did not know whether this was true of Patrick Balfour, but I expected that it might be. I had another reason for being on my guard. He had had affairs with two young women who had been concerns of mine. He had not 'cut me out'. They were warm-hearted ladies. Once he had followed, once he had anticipated my concern. In both cases there had been a time gap of at least a year. Even so it was possible that I might well come to resent their interest in him. It might have implied a criticism of myself.

In the 1890s Hubert Crackanthorpe wrote a story called 'A Dead Woman' in which a man discovers after his wife's death that she has been having an affair with his best friend. He goes to see his friend, hot for revenge but when he begins to talk to him, he finds that the love they shared with a dead woman is a bond between them, deepening their friendship. That can happen between two men who have been in love with the same woman at different times. But it can also happen that the knowledge of shared favours can cause deep dislike. What can she have seen in him? Perhaps she has got from him something that one could not give oneself.

One talks of 'possessing' a woman, but one knows, inside one's heart, that one has only touched a section of her, eighty per cent maybe, fifty per cent, even as little at times as thirty per cent, when one acts as stop-gap in her life. One knows that there is a part of her one has not touched. She is vulnerable, because of a deficiency in oneself, and there is nothing to be done about it.

One knows that she will sooner or later meet the man who will fill that deficiency. One loathes the man who can do just that. That is how it is quite often. But sometimes when there is a gap of time, and another man is filling the place one did in her life, one feels that she is attracted by the same things in him that had attracted her in oneself. That makes a bond.

I could not tell how it would be with Patrick Balfour. Would his association with those two women be a bond, or would I recognise that they had been attracted by characteristics antipathetic to me. Luckily the two passages were to prove a bond between us. I quite liked to think of them together.

Patrick was to become and was to remain one of my closest friends, the only real friend that Evelyn and I had in common. My meeting with him was one of the pleasantest of the many pleasant things that happened to me in 1931. I met him at a lucky time. He was in trouble of a temporary kind. An engagement had been broken off under circumstances which had convinced his father that he was heavily in debt and living beyond his means in London. His father had issued an ultimatum. 'I will pay your debts, if you will resign your job as Mr Gossip and go abroad quietly to work upon a serious book.' His father's idea of what was an adequate allowance for a young man writing a novel in the South of France was very different from what Patrick's had been three months earlier. Nor had Patrick any credit on the Riviera. He could not sign bills in restaurants. He was definitely poor and ready to welcome simple company.

Keith Winter, too, was poor. But in a different way. He was poor in the way that a quite prominent novelist very often is, when the finishing of the novel on which he will receive a large advance has been delayed and a couple of short stories that he had expected to sell right away to an American magazine have not yet found a market. Winter needed to lie low, but his position and his prospects were gilt-edged. His first novel *Other Men's Saucers* had attracted a great deal of attention. He had turned *The Rats of Norway* into a play with Laurence Olivier in the lead. He was twenty-four years old, he was friendly, pleasant looking; he gave himself no airs. Most people liked him, a rich future was prophesied for him. And for a few years his promise was abundantly fulfilled. His play *The Shining Hour* was a great success, on both sides of the Atlantic. Today he is forgotten. Something went wrong, somewhere, in Hollywood where things can so easily go wrong; and they went wrong in wartime, a difficult period for an Englishman far from his base. He had been discharged from the Navy, for ill health. There was nothing obvious for him to do in England. He received an offer from Hollywood. He took it and he has not come back. It is the kind of thing that happens in the world of letters. It is one of the reasons why writers do not encourage their children to make a career of authorship.

Shortly after the war, there was talk of M.G.M. filming *Brideshead Revisited*. Evelyn was summoned to Hollywood and installed in 'The Garden of Allah', at great cost to M.G.M. Keith Winter was requisitioned to write the script. Evelyn was told that Winter was in low waters and that he would be performing an act of kindness if he would be as co-operative as possible. A success now might restore his self-confidence. But Evelyn's heart was not in the deal. His income tax was so great that he would have received very little return from a sale to M.G.M. £150,000 would have become £1,500 and for so small a return he was not going to allow the meaning and message of his novel to be ruined by what Hollywood would call a happy ending with Charles Ryder marrying Julia. Moreover he was spending as much time as he could at Forest Lawns getting the material for *The Loved One*. On one occasion he was told that there was an important conference on the next day at the studio which he must attend. He was sorry, he said, he couldn't. 'But Mr Waugh,' he was informed by a breathless secretary, 'Mr Louis B. Meyer himself will be at the conference.'

'I can't help that,' he answered, 'at Forest Lawns they're laying out a stiff who's been two weeks in the water.'

In Villefranche, Evelyn had pretended that he was not on speaking terms with Winter, and that Winter must use Patrick as an intermediary when he wanted to address him. There was also some confusion about shirts. Winter had a red shirt with white spots that was only printed on one side of the linen. Winter was working in a room on the second floor, facing the Place du Marché. Whenever an acquaintance came on to the terrace, Evelyn would call up, 'Winter come out on the balcony and show these visitors your shirt.' There was also some long saga about, through a mistake at the laundry, Winter having appropriated Patrick's shirts. This saga of the shirt was continued in 'The Garden of Allah'. Winter arrived for lunch with Evelyn in an undervest, a jacket and no shirt. The head waiter would not allow Winter into the restaurant without a shirt, so that Evelyn had to go to a man's furnishing store and buy him one.

It was rumoured in England that Keith Winter had become a Roman Catholic. I have since heard that this is not true, but that he has found a 'purpose in life'; that he lives very simply in Greenwich Village, that he is devoted to 'good works' and that he is not unhappy, that he feels fulfilled. It is the last thing that I would have expected for him in that distant summer.

We all of us had friends along the coast, so that the family group often divided into separate parties. Patrick was an old friend of Somerset Maugham, and several visits were made to the Villa Mauresque; from one of these visits Patrick and Winter returned alone, having left the painter behind. 'Willie took a fancy to him,' Patrick explained. Next day the painter returned shortly before lunch with a well contented smirk. The great man, he told us, had been delighted with a trick of his with his finger tips that had reminded him of the boys in Bangkok. He felt he had been a great success and presumed that he would be invited to a number of W.S.M.'s smarter parties. But this was, in fact, the sole invitation that he received. I only once heard Maugham speak of him afterwards, and then it was on a derogatory note. 'Not a very agreeable person,' he remarked; yet I once saw them together that autumn at a small cocktail party given by Patrick Balfour. When the painter handed Maugham a glass the back of his hand touched Maugham's palm. As it did a lecherous expression came into Maugham's face, an expression I have only seen there that once. The incident is surely symptomatic. Robin Maugham has written that W.S.M. considered it one of his mistakes that he had tried to persuade himself that he was only twenty-five per cent homosexual, and seventy-five per cent heterosexual, whereas actually it was the other way about. I think he resented his own homosexual feelings and tried to despise, often with success, those who administered to them.

I see the painter every so often nowadays. He has been moderately successful. He is married; he has three children. He gives talks on the B.B.C. He has held two or three appointments in American universities. He is a popular member of the Savile.

In *Brideshead Revisited* Evelyn had the situation of a peer with a large estate, who during the first war deserted his wife, the mother of his four children and set up in Italy with another woman. He never returned to England, until, after his wife's death, he came home to die. That situation was suggested to Evelyn by an incident that took place that summer. One morning I found Evelyn and Patrick discussing over their coffee a report in the *Continental Daily Mail* that a divorce suit was being brought against one of the richest and most prominent peers of the realm, a man in his middle sixties who had been very active in political and public life. 'So the story has broken,' Evelyn said.

I will not mention the peer by name. I will use the name that was given him in Brideshead, Marchmain, with Flyte as the family name. In real life Lady Marchmain was the sister of a prominent Duke, and the case was being brought because of a quarrel between her husband and her brother, at her brother's instigation. A groom for whom Marchmain had formed an attachment many years before was to be cited. The case was never brought because the King intervened. He could not allow a man who had been his own representative to be exposed to scandal. But the case was only dropped on the condition that Marchmain left the country.

I had met Marchmain three months earlier in New York at a dinner party that F.D.R.'s mother had given for him. Both his sons had been Oxford contemporaries of Evelyn's. I had seen quite a lot of his younger son, and I exchanged a few words about him with his father. 'A dear dear boy,' he said. 'If only he would write to me more often.' The great man was very gracious and urbane, embellishing his role of guest of honour. He was on his way back from a world tour. Had he any knowledge of the trouble that awaited him in England?

His younger son was very good looking, very charming. He was also a very heavy drinker. He died young, through an accident, not through drink. When *Brideshead* was published it was generally assumed that he was the original of Sebastian Flyte.

Somerset Maugham often insisted that he himself rarely put real people into books – though in the end he did not deny that Alroy Kear was in large part Hugh Walpole, but when *Brideshead* was being discussed in the autumn of 1945 at a New York lunch party, he remarked, 'We all know, of course, who Sebastian was. A charming boy. He drank himself to death.'

But I should question whether he was more than casually in Evelyn's mind. Up to Evelyn's first marriage, I knew, or knew about, most of his friends, and I can recognise how much he took one feature here and one trait there. Charles Ryder is far from being a self portrait, and I would say that the role played by Sebastian in Ryder's life was filled in Evelyn's by Richard Pares and the Scot whom in *A Little Learning*, he calls Hamish Lennox. Hamish's mother, whom I never met was partly the original of Lady Circumference in *Decline and Fall*. Lady C. had a special wood port which was kept in plentiful supply and the consumption of Barford Port was the equivalent of the exuberant raids upon the Brideshead cellar. I wonder, incidentally, how many *Brideshead* readers were puzzled by Sebastian taking a bottle of Peyraguey on that first picnic. It was a hot day; there is no mention of ice, and Peyraguey is a very sweet Sauternes. It was one of Evelyn's idiosyncrasies to prefer his Sauternes unchilled. At one time he described it as 'White Claret'. The last time I dined at his house, he served in July a Sauternes at room temperature.

IX

I said in the first chapter of this book that fate vouchsafed me two romances in 1931. The second began during June. One morning as I was sitting on the terrace writing, with Evelyn beside me reading the *Eclaireur de Nice*, a taxi drove up to the hotel. From it stepped a young woman. She was alone. She had two suitcases. She was blonde. She was very thin. She was simply dressed in an ochre yellow sheath of linen. She moved with a lissom ease. Evelyn and I looked at each other. We knew exactly what each was thinking. 'Let's toss for it,' I said. 'A three day first refusal,' Evelyn suggested. I won the toss.

That evening I was sitting on the terrace with my parents and Keith Winter over a coffee and a *fine*: Evelyn and Patrick were in Nice. She strolled slowly along the waterfront. I stood up. 'I'm going to ask her to join us.' My mother suggested that it would be more proper if the invitation came from her. 'She probably only speaks French,' I said. But that was not so. She spoke English with an individual but educated accent. Her name was Mary G . . . She was a Canadian, she said. Her husband was an American, a painter. He was in Russia. He was going to join her here in a few days. They had a flat in Paris. She had two daughters. She was so slim that it was very hard to think of her as having daughters. She was very quiet, almost demure. I had not gained much by winning my bet, I thought.

Two evenings later, I had a small dinner party to which I invited her. During the previous day and a half I had scarcely seen her. She had not been to the beach. She had dined in Nice. She had gone in by bus. We had a short gossip by the Octroi, which was pleasant enough, but she had a remote air. Later she told me that at the time she was taking drugs. At the dinner – we were a party of six – she sat at the other end of the table. She looked very beautiful, but very abstracted. She did not take much part in the conversation, and I wondered if Evelyn would have better luck with her when my three days were up. We dined at what was then called the Cabanon and is now Jimmy's. After dinner we went to the Garden Bar. She sat against the wall, her head rested against it. She scarcely spoke, then, afterwards, as we walked back to the hotel, she slipped her hand into mine and pressed her sharp pointed nails into my palm. It was one of the most electric sensations of my life. In ten minutes we were in bed.

Many years later she was to say to me, 'If you want to get to know a man, you've got to go to bed with him.' I do not think she bothered to get to know a man, until she had been to bed with him.

Maugham makes a courtesan say in *The Razor's Edge*, 'It's the second night that counts,' and I have usually found that when the first night goes very well, it is never so good again, whereas the start of a serious affair is usually unsatisfactory. This was not so with Mary. I shall always remember tenderly that first night with her; but I shall always remember, with equal tenderness, the other nights we spent together. We never lost touch with one another; we became very good friends and whenever it seemed a good idea we made love together. The last time was in New York in the early 50s. She had a house in the country and had come in for a party. She was staying at the Algonquin. I was dining out. 'If you get back before half after eleven call me up,' she said. I took very good care to be back by quarter past.

The next evening we went into Nice. We had mint-juleeps in one of those quiet bars in which Nice abounds. Whereas before she had sat silent and secretive, now she chattered freely. I found that she was widely read, that she had an acute critical sense. She knew a great many painters. 'Binks (that was her nickname for her husband) has taught me what painting is. You teach me what writing is.' I was never to learn quite what she meant by that, but her criticisms of writers were always sound – even when they were destructive, which they often were. Twenty-four hours before I had had to 'make' conversation with her, now I was the listener. Twenty-four hours before, though I had admired her beauty as she had leant back against the wall of the Garden Bar, I had felt no impulse to put my arms round her; now I felt that I

109

could not face two hours of sitting opposite her across a dinner table. 'Let's get the barman to make us a sandwich,' I suggested. 'Let's picnic in the hotel'. I thought it would be romantic to drive back in an open *fiacre*. The twenty minutes beside her seemed unending.

Waiting for her in her letter box at the hotel was a green cable form. She pounced on it, she tore it open. 'Wonderful, wonderful,' she cried. 'Binks will be here tomorrow.' My heart sank. What cruel luck. When I was on the very brink of one of the best nights of my life. I need not have worried. It made no difference; but right through a long, long night she kept the cable form clenched in her left hand.

It was on the next morning that I took my parents to lunch in St Paul at the Colombe d'Or. We had meant to take Mary with us, but she preferred to spend the morning at the hairdressers in Nice, so that she should look radiant for her husband. My parents and I got back soon after six. As we walked down from the Octroi, the occupants of a taxi waved at us. Mary and her husband. He was, I recognised, a young painter who had been staying at the Welcome, the year before, and with whom I had become quite friendly.

There was another sartorial saga in addition to that of Keith Winter's shirts: Evelyn needed a pair of grey flannel trousers. It would have been simple for him to have got a pair at the Galeries Lafayette. But that, he said, he could not afford. He must get them on credit; so before leaving London he ordered a pair from his second grade tailors. It was his theory that a man should have two tailors, one for his urban clothes and country tweeds. The other for sports jackets, trousers and the like. He got his smart clothes from Anderson and Sheppard, but he had minor articles run up by a small Jewish tailor in the Charing Cross Road, from whom before coming out to France, he ordered a pair of grey flannel trousers with instructions that they were to be sent out to him. In those days a suit could be made within a week. It was an expensive and roundabout way of acquiring a simple object, but it was not unlike him to decline to pay cash and to refuse to wear a French garment. Seldom if ever can a project have been subjected to more delay. The trousers were in the first place sent to Paris instead of Villefranche. Customs duties had to be paid on them; the porter in his Paris hotel refused to pay them so the trousers were sent back to London. Evelyn telegraphed that the trousers were to be sent out by air. When eventually the trousers arrived, it was found that they did not fit. The entry for June 24 in my mother's diary reads, 'Left Villefranche 10.30 for Marseilles. Took Evelyn's trousers with us.' The extent of Evelyn's concern over the incident may be gauged by my mother's having bothered to mention it in a record that rarely contained as much as four lines a day.

The incident immersed Evelyn in gloom. He felt that there was a conspiracy against him. He had brought with him the manuscript of the travel book that was eventually published under the title *Remote Peoples*. He was not happy about it. He was rarely very happy about his travel books. He regarded them as hackwork. He made a book out of every long trip he took. I think this was a mistake. A single trip did not always provide him with as much material as he needed. After the war he condensed his three travel books into one *When the Going was Good*. It is infinitely better in my opinion than any one of the three separately. He was so dissatisfied with his last travel book, *A Tourist in Africa*, that he only sent copies to those who had helped him on his trip. My elder son Andrew who was A.D.C. to the Governor of Southern Rhodesia got a copy while I did not.

He had now come to feel he could not make the progress he needed with an uncongenial piece of work in The Welcome Hotel, with the various distractions provided by his parents, myself, Keith Winter, Patrick Balfour and the painter. He had heard of a monastery in Cabris where he could live for twenty-four francs a day, but he was short of money and could not afford to pay his hotel bill at the Welcome. He had asked his London agent to relieve the siege, but no funds had yet arrived. Another spearhead in the conspiracy. His gloom deepened. One morning I went into his room to find him stretched out on the bed, a leg hanging loose over the side: his hands under his head. He did not acknowledge my entrance, I went away. I returned an hour later to find that he had not moved. He was still staring at the ceiling. A family conference was held. It was clear that he must be got away from Villefranche. Unfortunately, I, too, was short of money. I had just enough to last me during the five days before I accompanied my parents back to England. In the end my father advanced him 1,500 francs.

My parents, though their resources were slender, were never without money. In the following April *Vile Bodies* was produced as a play in London. Evelyn had arranged a small supper party at the Savoy afterwards. At the last moment he found that he had reached the limits of his overdraft. He asked me for help. Two days before I had received a request from my bank not to issue any more cheques till my account had been placed in credit. In the end our mother came to our assistance. Our table at the Savoy was placed in the centre of the main room, away from the dancing floor. Ours was a gay party. I saw a good many heads turned in our direction. Evelyn and I must have seemed two fate-favoured mortals and so we were, yet we could not raise ten pounds between us.

On the afternoon of the day on which I finished *So Lovers Dream* my parents and I drove up to Chabris and left Evelyn in charge of the priests. It was very like seeing a small boy off to school. The monastery looked very dreary. That evening Binks caught the night train for Paris, leaving Mary behind. Neither of them seemed particularly depressed. I gathered that their marriage was nearing its close. 'He doesn't want the responsibilities that go with a home,' she said. 'He preferred the way it was in Russia, no servants, a studio in which to paint. I thought he would like a home.' I was very tempted to stay on in Villefranche. But I had a number of things to do in England. My novel had to be typed and corrected. I wanted to play some cricket. I also wanted to sit in the pavilion for the test match. 'But I'll come back the very first moment that I can,' I promised Mary.

X

On July 24th I started back for Villefranche. Quite a lot happened in those four intervening weeks. I soon became aware that England was not quite as safe and cosy as she had seemed when I read the Gossip columns in the *Continental Daily Mail* on the terrace of The Welcome.

Chapman and Hall was clearly in a financial plight, with the new managing director on the verge of a nervous breakdown. I was glad to think that I was no longer on the Board. I was also glad that I was no longer a Chapman and Hall author. As my own interests were not involved, I could be a very much better friend to my father. I could give him my full sympathy. I did not have to worry about how I should be affected personally.

My parents on their return decided to sell Underhill. It was too big for them, and a 'To Be Sold' notice-board went up by the front gate. It was a shock to see it there. Underhill had been my home since 1907. When I came back for the holidays, my father would put a placard in the grandfather clock 'Welcome Home to the heir of Underhill'. It had been my base since nursery days. Every return from school, from the Army, from my trips abroad had been made to Underhill. My parents would no doubt get themselves a flat where I could keep my clothes, where a spare room would be ready for me, but it would be different. Change was in the air.

I am surprised now that I did not realise how serious and widespread was this sense of change. The English tend to take things for granted; they concentrate on their personal and private problems and leave the conduct of public affairs to the professional politicians whom they have elected and the bureaucrats whose salaries they pay. But rereading Harold Nicolson's diaries for the years 1930–2, I am astonished how little I was aware of what was going on behind the scenes, and of how situations were being created by which in a year or two I was to be affected personally.

The menace of British fascism was one of the most disturbing features of the years 1933–9, and the preparations for that disturbance were being made during 1931. It cannot be denied that the failure of Sir Oswald Mosley's public life was one of the tragedies of the pre-war decade. Nigel Nicolson wrote among his prefaces to his father's diaries, '1931 was the year of the New party experiment. It is difficult for those who now associate Sir Oswald Mosley's name only with his headlong descent into fascism, with slogans chalked on a wall, to visualise the brilliant flowering of his youth. In 1931 he was thirty-five years old. Born the heir of a baronetcy, married to Lord Curzon's daughter – his marriage was attended by both the King of England and the King of the Belgians – handsome, rich, eloquent, determined, he frequently changed his party allegiance, but it did not hamper the growth of his reputation.' He was elected to Parliament in 1918 as a Conservative. He moved towards the left and sat as an Independent. Two years later he joined the Labour Party, and in June 1929 when Labour was again in power, Ramsay Macdonald appointed him Chancellor of the Duchy of Lancaster – with special responsibility for unemployment.

He appeared then the young man of destiny, but he was soon to find himself at 'outs with the party bosses'. He suggested in the Mosley manifesto a series of measures to relieve unemployment, including public utility schemes such as slum clearance and agricultural reconstruction, the stabilisation of prices through bulk purchase, the 'scientific' regulation of tariffs, the public control of banking and the expansion of home purchasing power. The remedies he suggested may well have been practicable. But he could not convince his immediate superior, J. H. Thomas, so he resigned from the Government and his place was taken by Clement Attlee. His speech of resignation made a great impression on the House. In October at the Party Conference he put his ideas forward in opposition to Ramsay Macdonald. He was only narrowly defeated. In January 1931 he returned to the attack at a special meeting of the Parliamentary Labour Party. In his *Life of George V* Harold Nicolson wrote, 'his speech was a success, but he insisted on a vote, and Arthur Henderson by deft compliments and appeals to solidarity and commonsense outwitted him'. His error robbed the country of a great parliamentarian: Mosely was now on his own. He was in Nigel Nicolson's phrase 'a formidable threat to all three major parties from whom he hoped to attract many recruits': all the leaders wanted to have him on their side – Lloyd George, Churchill, the Conservatives, the Liberals, all courted him. Beaverbrook and Rothermere both considered giving him their support. The trouble was that he was not prepared to serve under any one. He insisted on running his own show.

I never met Mosley. I only once saw him at a meeting that he addressed in Basingstoke. In was in 1937 or 1938. By then he was in the wilderness, and in what his father-in-law had warned him against, 'ineffective isolation'. He had a strong platform personality and was an effective speaker. But to me he seemed unlikeable; I suppose that was his tragedy. No first class man was ready to work with him for long. John Strachey left him in mid-1931. Harold Nicolson left him early in the following year.

On July 1st, I played my first match as a member for MCC. It was against Felstead School. I read in my father's diary that I took seven wickets for thirty-eight. I have no recollection of the game itself, but I do remember that S. H. Saville was on the side. He had been as a Middlesex cricketer one of the heroes of my youth. In August 1910 at Lords when Middlesex, set 242 to win by Essex, had lost eight wickets for 140, he and P. F. Warner had hit off the remaining hundred in an hour. As I had watched him from the mound with the sun slanting from behind the professionals' pavilion and a match card stuck under my straw hat to protect my eyes, I had little guessed that twenty-one years later, I should be going out to field beside him.

The test match for whose sake I had returned was against India, and proved disappointing: India was very weak. But I spent two enjoyable days watching the Oxford and Cambridge match. It was a surprising game. For Cambridge, A. T. Ratcliffe by scoring 201 broke J. F. Marsh's record of 171 that had stood for fifty years; the very next afternoon the Nawab of Pataudi scored

238 and on the following day Oxford won by eight wickets, their first win since 1923.

On the Sunday before the match began I went down to Oxford to lunch with the Willerts. It was an occasion that was to have consequences for me. I met there Inez, the younger daughter of Walters of *The Times*. She was sixteen years old. She was dark, highly attractive, with an Oriental air. It was one of the few sunny afternoons that summer, and we sat on the lawn discussing modern poetry. I made, she was to tell me later, a considerable impression on her because I was the first adult who had treated her on equal terms. We were to meet often over the years. She was in Cairo during the war; her husband – she is now Lady Burroughs – was a diplomat. I remember a small cocktail party of hers that was attended by King Farouk. Later in Washington she was to extend much hospitality to me. My meeting with her was one of the many incidents in 1931 that was to make me look back on that year gratefully.

There was a second corollary to my meeting with Inez Walters – one that had a big effect on my parents' lives and consequently on mine. Inez Walters had a married sister, Mrs O'Neil. I cannot remember whether she was there that day or whether I learnt from Inez that she had a one-year-old poodle for which she was trying to find a home. My parents had had a poodle all their married life. They were now looking for another. I put my parents in touch with Mrs. O'Neil. On the 21st of July she came, bringing 'Tuppence'. My parents were delighted with him and retained him. His arrival altered my parents' life in this, that they became so devoted to him that they felt they could not leave him with a vet when they went on their annual holiday. They decided that in future they must go somewhere that they could take him with them. So they picked on a hotel boarding house in Worthing. This meant that they never went to France again. It was the break of a routine for us. My father missed France. When the train pulled out of Calais or Boulogne, a broad grin would cross his face. 'France all round me, happy, happy, happy', he would say. He had become so conditioned to going to France every June or July that when the summer began, he would often start breaking into French – a language he scarcely spoke.

Tuppence was one of the three best of the poodles that we had – we had six in all – and when he had to be put down in November 1941, my mother felt that she was too old to start the training of another. She was afraid that after a few years she would not be strong enough to take him on the long walks over the heath that his health required.

He was a loving and much loved dog. Mrs O'Neil used to visit him once a year. She had taught him when he was a puppy to jump on her knees and place his paws upon her shoulders. When she came to see us he would always, the moment she had sat down, jump on her knees and perform his trick. He never did this with anybody else. My mother was rather jealous.

In mid-July I went to Surrey for J. C. Squire's annual cricket tour. It was to last ten days. It was the fourth such tour I went on. Usually it was one of the best weeks in the year. Squire had a house at Bowler's Green. He used to put up two or three players in his own house. The others he put up in a local pub, or housed with local friends. Sir Edward Marshall Hall's widow had a large house nearby. She was a German woman, I fancy Jewish, of considerable wealth. Squire always arranged that Ralph Straus should be her guest. It seemed to him that an appropriate marriage could be arranged, but Straus preferred his independence.

We had a mixed fixture list. We played against one or two very rural villages, but there was one match against the R.A.O.C., at Aldershot. Here we were playing out of our class, but once we managed to beat them. We played once at Tichborne Park, a village side but a beautiful ground with a good pitch, and at Fernden against a side got up by my old preparatory school headmaster N. G. Brownrigg, on the school ground.

I have written elsewhere about Squire's captaincy. He is the Mr Hodge of A. G. Macdonnell's *England, Their England*. The description of the village match in it has become a classic. It depicts a very typical invalids match.

Squire paid all the expenses of his team. When he was in funds he was most generous. Too many people today remember him as he was in the late 30s and the 40s, improvident and ill-kempt, always anxious to raise a small loan. He was in low waters in 1931, but he went on living as though he were still affluent. I believe I am correct in saying that in the early 20s he paid the university fees of two men who became highly prominent later on. John Gross in his *The Rise and Fall of the Man of Letters* gives a sad picture of his declining years: 'after giving up the editorship of the *London Mercury* in 1934 he drifted further and further into a semi-vagrant existence; he was saved from the worst by his work as a reader for Macmillan's and a reviewer for the *Illustrated London News*, and by the kindness of various women friends, but for the most part his life was a chaos of unpaid bills and unfulfilled commitments. He was once reduced to telling an editor that his manuscript had been blown out of the window of a taxi while he was on his way to deliver it.'

During the later 1920s, a number of his friends made strenuous efforts to organise his finances. He was making a reasonable amount of money; a bank would have been prepared to settle his debts in return for a monthly liquidation of his indebtedness. An organised budget was all that was needed. Surely a very simple thing. But no one could control his improvidence, his enthusiasm for new projects, his addiction to the bottle. Only once did he make a serious attempt to pull himself together, in the late summer of 1928. It was an attempt worthy of his eccentricity, of his refusal to admit that anything was impossible. As August was working to a close, and soccer was making its inroads into the last days of the cricket season, he murmured, 'What I wouldn't give to play one more game of Rugger.' H. S. Mackintosh overheard him. Mackintosh had been a contemporary of mine at Sherborne. He was a successful business man, who made quite a name for himself, as a writer of light verse, ballades in particular. 'There's no reason why you shouldn't' he said. 'It's only a question of getting into training.'

'I'm forty-four.'

'But your heart's all right. Let's see what my father says.'

Mackintosh's father was a doctor. He entered into the conspiracy. There was no reason why Squire should not return to the football field, if he went into solid training, if he gave up alcohol and smoking and took regular exercise, in gradually increased doses. Mackintosh proposed Squire as a member of the Rosslyn Park R.F.C.; this entitled him to wear a red and white striped jersey. Clad in this, he would three times a week in the early evening run up and down the lawn of Mackintosh's Hampstead garden, passing a Rugby football back and forth. 'The first week we'll have a thirty minutes practice; the second week forty minutes, the third week fifty. After a month we'll see how you are making out. In the meantime no smoking, and no alcohol.' The claims of a family, the sacred trust of poetry, his obligations to the *London Mercury*; these he could resist, but the hope of playing Rugby football forced him into temperance. It was all of it very typical of Squire. Mackintosh treated him as Laban had treated Jacob. He continually postponed the fulfilment of Squire's hopes. 'Another week, Jack, I think. We should make it in another week.' Then when the week was past, once again he would shake his head. 'You don't want to spoil it all by playing before you're ready.' From mid-August to mid-October the evening practices continued. By then it became too dark for practices after a day's work. 'Never mind,' said Mackintosh, 'There are the week-ends, a double dose on Saturday and Sunday.' But on Saturday Jack had to finish the article for the *Observer* that he always left to the last moment. 'It'll have to be Saturday afternoon.'

For ten weeks the treatment continued. Then the weather broke. The Saturday run up and down the lawn had to be postponed. It was still raining on the Sunday, then Mackintosh's firm sent him overseas for three weeks. Squire could scarcely have been expected to stay in training without the goad of that football being passed from hand to hand.

On his first day back in London, Mackintosh found Squire in the Savile in a state of post-prandial stupor. 'No good, Hugh old boy,' he muttered, 'too old for football. Have to stick to cricket.' As far as I know he never again abandoned the habits of a life-time.

He was at his best on his cricket tours. He was boyish and light hearted. He never gave himself any airs. Even the rain did not damp his spirits during those ten days. I remember that I had a thoroughly good time on that cricket tour, because I was with friends, but the cricket was ruined by the rain; it was an appalling summer. I cannot recall the details of a single game. My father came down to watch the game at Fernden. His joining us is the only thing about the game that I remember. His diary records, 'Alec made a duck.'

That night we dined in Farnborough, at the old coaching inn. The evening broke up, as every Invalids' dinner did with the singing of that old song from 'The Arcadians':

> It'll be all the same, all the same
> a hundred years from now.
> No use a worrying, no use a hurrying
> no use a kicking up a row.
> It'll be all the same, all the same
> when a hundred years have gone,
> Somebody else will be well in the cart
> and the world will still roll on.

During the tour I shared a room in the local pub with Eric Gillett. I had brought with me the manuscript of *So Lovers Dream* and he asked if he could read it. Eric Gillett was and still is one of my closest friends. He is three years older than I, but we were raised in the same stable. He was at Radley, which is one of Sherborne's rivals and had been in the XI in 1913, the year before I was in the Sherborne side. He had planned to go to Oxford, to Lincoln College, but the war stopped that and in October 1916 he was very badly wounded on the Somme in the hip and leg. Today those wounds cause him a great deal of pain and inconvenience. But they did not prevent him in the 20s from being an agile cricketer. At Hockey he kept goal. On Clifford Bax's cricket tours he was nicknamed 'Jumbo' – because he recounted an incident of two venerable military figures opening an innings in the last hour of the first day in a two-day match, 'Well Jumbo, old boy,' said one of them, 'shall we go in and play for keeps.' I do not know why it should have seemed funny but it did. And the nickname was appropriate. He had an elephantine quality which has increased with the years as he has put on weight and the limp from his wound has grown more pronounced. I met him first in August 1921, when he came on Clifford Bax's Newbury cricket tour. He had met Arnold Bax in Switzerland, and Bax enrolled him in the side. It was surprising how many members of the side had, after the war, been enrolled by Arnold Bax who never seemed to go anywhere and, as far as I know, hardly ever entertained, whereas Clifford was a social person.

When Gillett joined Clifford's side, he was still at Oxford. He took a little while to find himself in the post-war world. For a time he was warden of a college in Birmingham. Then he married and accepted a post as a lecturer in Singapore University. We all thought that he had gone for good. Clifford used to publish every Christmas a small volume containing the scores of the previous summer. The accounts of the matches were written by different members of the sides, some of them were really rather good and A. D. Peters' account of a match in the manner of Damon Runyan was printed in a cricket anthology edited by Denzil Batchelor. In the account of a match in July 1926, Clifford Bax wrote of Gillett playing a sterling innings of over fifty 'in probably his last match for us on the eve of his departure for Singapore'. But he was back within three years, as exuberant as ever, resolved to make his mark in the world of publishing. He has not been by any means unsuccessful. He has written reviews, he has talked on the B.B.C., he has worked for two publishing houses. He has done a fair amount of editorial work. He is someone of whom most people in the literary world have heard. He is well liked and he is respected. He is a familiar figure both at Lord's and at the Sussex Cricket Ground at Hove.

He gave me very valuable advice about my novel. When he was half way through, he said, 'This is really two books you know. It's a love story that explains the problems of a contemporary writer when he falls in love, but it also presents a picture of America today which is independent of that story.'

'I must reread it with that in view.'

When I did, I recognised that he was absolutely right. As I wrote in an earlier chapter, I had had two things on my mind

121

when I set down to write the book; I wanted to write about Ruth, and I wanted to describe what I felt about America. In its own way America's impact on me was as much a *coup de foudre* as my romance with Ruth. As I had first seen America and Ruth simultaneously, I had felt that the two emotions ran side by side. The one enhanced, explained and intensified the other; and if I had recounted my romance as it had actually happened, and the heroine of the novel had actually been Ruth, I might have run the two issues into one, but because I had altered both Ruth's character and the setting of the plot, I had written two separate books, a story and a treatise. On revision I removed about twelve thousand words that had no bearing on the central story, in the hope of using them in the future.

The novel was immensely improved by Eric Gillett's criticism. I have often read in dedications, a novelist's tribute to the help that he has received from editors. The case of Maxwell Perkins and Thomas Wolfe is quoted by practically every professor of creative writing. But personally I have only three times been helped by criticism. On this occasion by Eric Gillett, in 1929 by A. D. Peters, who suggested a different ending for a light modern-girl novel called *Sir, She Said*, and a few years ago my New York agent Carol Brandt saved my erotic comedy *A Spy in the Family*. As one or two readers of these pages may remember, a young married woman on a holiday in Malta is seduced by a German lesbian. On her return to England she finds that the German was an agent in a drug traffic concern. The heroine's encounter with her had been taped, and the heroine was forced by the threat of blackmail to smuggle heroin into England. This opening section occupied 100 pages. It was my original plan to show the London branch of this blackmail group operating on several other victims, so that I should have had three distinct stories interwoven. I intended a novel of some hundred thousand words. I showed the first 100 pages to Carol Brandt with a synopsis of the remainder. She shook her head. 'No, no,' she said. 'Stick to your one heroine. You are very unlikely to find another character as interesting as she is.' I did not see her point at first. In my previous novels I had exploited the technique of interwoven plots. 'And that,' she said, 'was why your last one (*The Mule on the Minaret*) didn't do as well as we had hoped. The reader was puzzled at being switched from one set of characters to another. Stick to your one character this time. She's vivid and interesting.'

'That means a very short novel doesn't it.'

I had formed the idea that I was not good enough to write a short novel, that I had to impress by bulk.

She shook her head. Sixty thousand words that grip the reader are better than a quarter of a million that confuse him.'

I had the good sense to follow her advice. My erotic comedy is a mini-book. It is not for all palates, and it shocked, surprisingly enough, the fiction editor of *Playboy*, but it has had on the whole a very satisfactory reception, particularly as a paperback. I think it is my best-told story.

On my return from Bowler's Green I found Evelyn in the Savile. He was preparing to leave for France the following day. He had finished *Remote Peoples* in his monastery and was in funds again. 'In that case,' I said, 'could you lend me thirty pounds?' Once again I had reached the limits of my overdraft. I should get an advance from Cassell's on the delivery of *So Lovers Dream* but that was two weeks away and I did not want to borrow from Peters before I had to. 'Certainly,' he said, 'I'll make you a cheque out right away.' But at that moment the porter called him to the telephone. He was away five minutes. He returned, smiling. 'I'm afraid that I shan't be able to lend you that thirty pounds after all. A young female has decided to accompany me to the South of France.'

I never learnt her name, but the sequel to the incident I heard later from Patrick Balfour. She was an ex-debutante of twenty-three, and she enjoyed what she called 'brinking', going as near as possible to the line without crossing it. Evelyn had a look of innocence, and she expected to be able to keep him dangling, but she very soon found that without a bestowal of ultimate favours she would have to find her way home alone. She shrugged. If that was what he wanted, well he must have it, but he should have so much of it that he would wish he had not brought the matter up.

She insisted on prolonged siestas. For propriety's sake, though that is not necessary in France, they had different rooms; at night she would not let him go back to his room till two or three and in the early mornings, at first light, she would bound into his room, eager and voracious. To her surprise and later to her considerable pleasure, she was accorded an appreciatively appropriate welcome. On the second morning, she was thinking, 'This is too good to miss a minute of.'

'Don't you think, Evelyn, that it would be easier if we shared a room?' she said.

My return to Villefranche was delayed by a Royal Command to attend a Garden Party at Buckingham Palace. I was as surprised as I was delighted to receive the impressively embossed card of invitation. I could not think why I had been thus honoured. I had never been to a levée and during the last five years I had spent so much time abroad that I had lost any claim that I might have possessed in 1925 to being a 'figure about town'. But there it was; the embossed card was proudly erected on the mantelpiece and the night before I supped at the Savoy so that I could get my silk hat ironed in the cloak room. Very few men, if any, wore grey hats in those days, but I wore a silk hat for lunch on Sundays and two or three times a week in the evening. Every month or so, I would get it ironed at the Savoy, giving the attendant a shilling instead of the customary sixpence.

Thursday July 23 was one of the few completely fine days that summer. Cricket was played everywhere. As I sauntered from the Park Lane tube station I noticed how the traffic was being redirected. This was on my account, I smugly told myself. I thought of all the people who were being inconvenienced because certain selected subjects of the Crown had been bidden to saunter under the Palace trees. It made me feel very important.

That was my chief sensation throughout the afternoon – a sense of self-importance. But it was in itself a highly enjoyable occasion. I had not been to very many garden parties. Weddings in the country and fêtes on rectory lawns were the extent of my experience. I read next morning in *The Times* that several thousand guests had been entertained. But there was no sense of being crowded. I did not have to queue up for my iced coffee, my strawberries and ice cream. In the distance I saw Their Majesties moving among the guests. I did not know a great many people there. I recognised more people than I knew. I was amused to see a start of surprise on the face of a fashionable lady whom I had met once or twice at the Hansards in Cadogan Gardens and who clearly had not expected to see me there. I encountered the St John Ervines. That pleased me. They were two of the first friends I made in London after the war. I liked them very much. They were important figures in the literary scene. I was always flattered when I received an invitation from them. Their presence at the party increased my self-esteem. I could see now what had happened. Royalty had felt that it should honour literature so it had selected a special group of youngish writers of distinction – people like the Ervines and myself. Then I detected a rather ostentatious poetaster who edited a very little magazine which did not pay its contributors. A very second-rate figure on the fringe. Why on earth had he received an invitation? I did not feel quite so well about my own. He greeted me with what I thought excessive cordiality. I barely knew him. I could imagine him in the future coming up to me at some publisher's gathering and remarking over loudly, 'I haven't seen you since last year's Royal Garden Party.'

My spirits were cheered, however, by the eagerness with which a couple of very young and attractive girls hurried over to me, Betty Askwith and Theodora Benson. I had met Theodora two years before when I was lecturing in the midlands. Her parents had a house in the neighbourhood, and my hostess had asked her to lunch to meet me. I can still see her walking across the lawn to join us. She was very slim, very tall; because of her height she walked with a slight stoop. She was wearing a well-cut tailored coat and skirt. She was then at the start of her career. I do not remember anything she said. Later I was to find her one of the funniest women I have ever known. But she was shy and silent on this occasion. I did not know much about her work. All I did know was that she wrote books in collaboration with Betty Askwith. A little later she wrote to tell me that she and Betty had been reading with interest my novel about young girls, *Sir, She Said*. They would like to discuss it with me. Would I come to tea with them?

Theodora was quite different when she was with Betty. I have never known a couple who were so much a team. They talked together as though there were one person; then they became separate and were two. It was fascinating. They had great youthfulness, and a deep, deep innocence. I asked them if they found it difficult to write in collaboration. Did each have her special set of characters? They shook their heads; no, they talked out the dramatic scenes together. 'We take it in turns as to who describes the kisses.' I thought that very touching. That autumn they published *Lobster Quadrille*, with Grant Richards. They had a celebration party, at, I think, Theodora's house. There were about eight of us. We went after a light meal to a musical. I do not remember its name, but I remember two of the songs, 'The Party's Getting Wild' and 'I Won't Leave My Bachelor Days Till My Bachelor Days Leave Me'. After the show we went back to Theodora's home for a drink and a sandwich. Grant Richards, who must by then have been nearly sixty, looked as spruce and immaculate at the end of the evening as he had at the beginning. He was a great charmer.

That was in November 1930. I had not seen Betty and Theodora since.

Meeting them at the Royal Garden Party was a reunion and it proved to be the beginning of a new deep friendship with the two, with Betty in particular. When I had met her first, I had had that quick feeling of recognition that I have nearly always had when I have met a woman who is likely to mean something to me. A very slight flicker, though. Now seeing her a year later with all the difference that a year can make in a young girl, seeing her smile under a wide floppy hat, I felt that flicker again only this time much more strongly. Something had begun.

There were three chairs vacant in the shade. We sat on them. The talk moved easily, intimately. 'When are you coming to tea with us again?' asked Theodora.

'Soon.'

'Take out your diary and tell us when,' she said.

'Alas, I leave for Villefranche tomorrow.'

'Oh.'

There was a silence.

'What are you doing this evening?' Betty asked.

'I'm dining with A. D. Peters.'

'And afterwards?'

'Victor Gollancz is giving a party.'

'We're going to it.'

'Then we'll meet there.'

Peters was at that time living in Southwick Street. It was a small dinner, a pre-party dinner. It was one of those occasions that means little at the time, but acquire significance in the light of what is to happen later. I recall this dinner party in particular because it was the last time that I was to dine with the Peters' as a team. Their marriage broke up that autumn.

There was nothing that evening to suggest that their life together was not a cordial one. I was very fond of his wife Helen; I had been present when they met, in March 1920, at dinner at W. L. George's. She was not particularly pretty, though she was nice looking. She had a supple figure, but what struck me about her most was the way she gesticulated as she talked. She had fascinating wrists. It had been a foggy night and Peters had seen her home. Early the following summer, he brought her to the Hampstead Cricket Ground to watch a game in which we both were playing. A man like Peters who tended to divide up his life in water-tight compartments did not bring a woman to watch cricket unless he had designs. I was not surprised when they married in the autumn.

I was to see as much of them as I was of any couple during the twenties; I was always cheered at a party when I saw them there. They spread conviviality. They were a team. I imagine that she must have been helpful to him professionally. He was reserved. He found it difficult to be encouraging. His phlegmatic manner was most effective when things were going badly. I would think, 'I have a lot to get off my chest. I must have a long, long talk with

Peters'. I would begin to pour out my problems. He would sit like a great Buddha, saying nothing. In face of his silence I would dry up slowly. I thought I had enough material to last half an hour. I would find I had finished within five minutes. He would stir in his chair. 'I don't think you've anything to worry about,' he would say. 'I guess you want a change of air. Why not take ten days in Nice? Cassell's would advance you fifty pounds, I'm sure. If they won't, I can.'

He was wonderful when things were going badly, but he was not encouraging when the wheel of fortune turned. Enthusiasm was not his long suit. That was where Helen was invaluable. She would give his clients the sense of being appreciated that Peters often failed to do. I remember her saying to me in 1927 when I had returned from a trip round the world, 'Peter was really excited by those stories you sent back from Siam. He said "This trip has made Alec a new writer."' It was so exactly what I needed to hear. I imagine that she filled the same role for others of his clients. On this particular evening, she and Peters seemed as pleased as ever with each other: one in a long succession of such evenings.

The other special reason that I have for remembering that party is that I met A. J. Cronin. He had just published *Hatter's Castle*. It was having an immense success. He was a man of thirty-five who only a year before had abandoned medicine – in which he was having a distinguished career. He was married with, at that time, two children. He had run an immense risk in giving up his practice. He must have had supreme self-confidence. I would have expected him to have an overbearing 'after all I told you so' manner. He could not have been more different. He was tall, handsome; he had a presence that must have given him a good bedside manner. But what struck me most about him was his modesty. It was not in any way, a diffidence. It was an un-assumingness. He gave himself no airs, when it would have been very natural if he had. I hoped that I should see a good deal of him. But as it happened I only saw him once more, for a brief moment at one of Heinemann's big parties.

He has now made his home in Switzerland, after spending

several years in the U.S.A. He was there during the war; and possibly he may directly afterwards have had qualms about returning to a changed England, as did several actors who had spent the war in Hollywood. There was at that time a captious atmosphere of self-righteousness about some Britons who themselves had had no opportunity of doing anything but stay where they already were. They argued that any Briton who was not sent abroad on His Majesty's Service, should make his contribution to the war effort, inside his own country. In Cronin's case it was argued that as he had been a doctor, he should have put his medical skill at his country's service. This was a foolish argument. Cronin had retired ten years earlier. He would be out of touch with the latest ideas; his eye would be out, his hand would be out. He would be unlikely to receive an important appointment; the mandarins of the medical profession had not forgiven him for *The Citadel*. He would almost certainly have been found employment of some kind, but it would not have been of the kind he would have received had he remained a practicising surgeon through the 30s; of course, it would have been work of national importance, and it would have been performed in uniform. But in 1930 he had thought that writing not medicine was his true bent, and he was entitled to go on thinking that in 1939.

In World War I, it had been felt by the young that there was no alternative to front-line service. Raymond Asquith declined a staff appointment, because he felt that he could not desert his troops and sit at a desk behind the lines in comparative safety. He was honoured for his refusal. In the second war, with commando raids and saturation bombing, there was no such thing as 'comparative safety'. Moreover it was recognised that there were such things as 'a reserved occupation'. Schoolmastering for instance. In the first war the youth of the nation suffered through sitting under old and inefficient teachers. Not so in the second war. In 1939 authorship, too, was considered a reserved occupation. Many British writers found employment in some form or other of publicity and propaganda, and, not surprisingly in view of the small number of writers who are able to support themselves by their pens alone, welcomed the opportunity of taking a salaried

129

post. I myself, as a lieutenant in the Regular Army Reserve of officers was recalled to my regiment in the first week of the war. I was glad to take a long breather in mid-stream. But if a writer felt himself capable of continuing his career of authorship during the war, he was entitled to do so, because writing is in itself important. Cronin at a base hospital could have done very useful service with a syringe, but the pen is a mightier weapon. No one should deny the value of morale, and Cronin's *The Keys of the Kingdom* published in 1945 must have fortified the faith of many soldiers and war workers. He would not have been better employed writing hand-outs at the Ministry of Information.

A social friend informed me that it was correct after being invited to Buckingham Palace to sign the book there. So on the following day she drove me through the guarded gate and showed me where to sign. In the afternoon I caught a train for the South of France. I was due at Nice at half-past seven the following night. It was not one of the great trains, and I should have half an hour's wait in Marseilles. I had with me the final corrected typescript of *So Lovers Dream*. I would read it for the last time on the way down, then post it in Marseilles.

My heart was light as I walked back to my carriage. My decks were cleared. Cassell's had two manuscripts of mine. I did not need to bother about work while the summer lasted. How good to be master of my own time; to be able to concentrate all that time on Mary; to have nothing except her to think about; she would be waiting on the platform for me. How long would I be staying there? I did not know. I did not care. Perhaps we might take a trip together. To Corsica? Why not? Never before had the immediate future seemed more full of promise. For nearly a year I had been working at full pressure. Two complete novels and a lecture tour. Now I could reap my reward.

It did not turn out that way. I had been away a month and during that month the summer season had begun. There was no question now of the Welcome's kitchen being closed. The hotel was crowded, and you had to have full pension whether or not you had your meals elsewhere. The round blue tables on the terrace were requisitioned by other breakfasters. As usual I was the first there. But I could not have stayed on after I had finished my roll and coffee, even if I had had a *cahier* to linger over. The fact that I had not, made a vast difference. The mornings had passed quickly when I was composing my daily contribution of three thousand words. S. N. Behrman once said: 'If you have done three hours writing the rest of the day takes care of itself.' Had I had work to do I could have done it in my bedroom, as I had on my first visit two years before. But I had no work; there was a lack of anywhere to sit and read, except the beach. There is a limit to the amount of time you can spend in the sun, and the beach at Villefranche is uncomfortable. Pebbles instead of sand, and it was hard to find a point in the wall below the railway line from which a stone did not project.

It was not only Villefranche that was crowded. The whole coast was. Residents like Eldred Curwen were caught up by a full tide of entertainment. There were parties every night. There always had been since the summer vogue for the South of France had started, but in early years Villefranche had seemed cut off from the main traffic of the coast. It had seemed an island, but now the invading tide had encroached upon its solitude. Edward Wasserman had taken Paul Morand's villa, the Orangerie. He had invited Harold Acton as a house guest. A friend of his had brought his yacht into the harbour. There was a restless atmosphere along the waterfront. There was a constant coming and going. This atmosphere was quickened by the inauguration of a line of coaches that ran straight from Nice into the square. The old trolleys that stopped at the Octroi had been discontinued. These buses were a great convenience. They saved one the long pull up the hill on a hot morning, but Villefranche was no longer a place apart.

This social animation was, of course, a great deal of fun. A number of amusing people had come south for their holidays. Lady Willert was at the Cap. I met and became friends with Edward Sackville West. Harold Acton added gaiety to every party. But it was not the same Villefranche that it had been during the early summer, not was it the same Villefranche that it had been two years earlier when Berta Ruck and her two sons had been there.

But perhaps I should not have been so conscious of the change in Villefranche if Mary herself had been the same. A lesson I have never seemed to learn is that you cannot leave a woman for four weeks and find her unchanged on your return. Often absence makes a man's heart grow fonder, because he is transferred to a masculine occupation, a business trip, a safari or a cricket tour; there is no woman in his life. But a woman remains in her same feminine atmosphere: doing precisely the same things that she was before, only without a man. There is a gap, that she needs to fill. She has not, as the man has, moved into a world of new interests that keep her occupied.

That is how it was with Mary. I had been missing her, more and more. Whereas she . . . About a week after I had left her she had been sitting alone on a chair in front of The Welcome. One of the Villefranche boys – Benito – walked slowly past her. He was neatly dressed. He was handsome. He had black hair. He had an Italian look. When the war broke out, it was found that he really was Italian. He crossed the frontier before Italy joined the war. He never came back to Villefranche. No one knows what happened to him. He was gracious. He had charming manners. He did not work. He supported himself on the presents that he received from women, and from men.

A minute later he returned. He was walking more slowly now. He paused in front of Mary. 'You are alone,' he said. 'It is sad to be alone.' He smiled. 'May I sit down,' he said. She nodded. He said he would like a coffee. 'Why not come in with me to Nice?' he said. They were to spend several afternoons in Nice.

She was there to meet my train. We dined at one of the one-storied restaurants on the Quai des Etats-Unis. A musician played to us from the pavement. The air was warm. This time I was too impatient to take a *fiacre* back. We went straight to her room. It was a delight to be with her again. But it was different. She was different. Those afternoons in Nice had made her different.

She was also exceedingly depressed. When I saw her first there was a large bruise on her hip. She told me that she had fallen out of a taxi in Paris. Later she told me that she had tried to commit suicide. At that period every two months she attempted to commit suicide. The mood was about to come to full cycle. She was also taking drugs. She would sit at a table without speaking. An abstracted look would be on her face. She did not seem to be listening to the conversation. She looked ethereal. 'Was I very beautiful in those days?' she was to ask me a few years ago. 'Yes, you were very beautiful.' 'But I wasn't happy you know. I'm much happier now, though I am fat and ugly.'

The news from Paris heightened her despondency. Her marriage was clearly near its end. She had been excited when Binks came back from Russia. They had seemed very cordial together. But he was dissatisfied with domesticity. He disliked the responsibility of running a household. He preferred the casual atmosphere of studios. She ran a house well. In 1934 when she was divorced, I was surprised to find how tidy her New York house was and how well her children were turned out. She said pathetically but not self-pityingly, 'I gave him a comfortable home. I thought that was what he needed. But it doesn't seem to be.'

Had I known her better, I would have recognised that she was on the edge of a crisis. It came without warning. Fred McEvoy's mother had rented a small house in Villefranche. Her younger son was staying with her. He was a lively, healthy young man. He often joined us at The Welcome's bar. He had a motor cycle. One evening he collided with a car at the junction of the roads before Cap Ferrat. His arm had to be taken off. Within half an hour the news had reached The Welcome. 'It isn't true, tell me it isn't true,' said Mary.

'As far as I know it is.'

'I can't bear it. I can't. I can't.'

She got up from the table, leaving her drink unfinished. She did not come back to it. Next morning she was not around. In those days the rooms did not have telephones. I went to the beach without her. When I returned shortly before noon, the desk reported that she had not been seen downstairs, and that she had not rung for breakfast. I tapped on the door. There was no answer. I tried the handle. The door was locked. I wondered if she had gone out and taken her key with her. She might have done. I did not worry then but I did when there was no sign of her at dinner. I walked to the far side of the jetty. Her window was shuttered. There was no light showing through the chinks. Next morning I told the proprietor. He agreed that we should have to find out if anything was wrong. He had a pass-key which if the key was still in the lock, could push it out. I went up with him, and with his wife. Mary was lying on the counterpane, unconscious and completely naked.

We took her to the hospital. She did not recover consciousness until after midnight. She was in a room with several beds. A nurse, a nun, was reading by candlelight. Mary had been brought up as a Catholic; she had hated her schooldays. Roused out of her barbituric daze, she imagined she was imprisoned, with a nun guarding her; back in her convent. She jumped out of bed, ran out of the room, crossed a corridor, opened the door of the room opposite. It was in part a military hospital. It was into a male ward that she had broken. A couple of bearded *poilus* roused from their sleep were startled to see an exquisite and naked nymph climbing on to the sill. They thought that they had entered paradise. They were sick, recovering from injuries. But they had the presence of mind to rescue her. The incident caused a considerable amount of mirth in the Welcome's bar, but it caused concern to the hotel management. It did not improve the hotel's credit to have its guests attempting suicide. Mary was told that her room was no longer available. Her suitcases were already packed and in the porter's charge. Should the porter carry them to another hotel? Mary shook her head. She thought she would like to try Cap Ferrat. She mentioned the name of a hotel. Perhaps the proprietor would be so kind as to ring up and ask if it had a vacant room. Standing beside her desk, I remembered that a good looking man who had joined us two nights before on The Welcome Terrace had told us that he was on holiday in that hotel.

Mary took her expulsion with equanimity. She might just as well be in Cap Ferrat as in Villefranche, particularly in view of the young man's presence there. But it made a very marked difference to me. The ten days since my return had not been the honeymoon I had expected, but even so without Mary I should be at a loose end in Villefranche. There was nothing that I felt a need to write. The mornings would be slow in passing. I was not tempted to cross to Cap Ferrat. Mary had not suggested that I should. I suspect that she had got a little bored with me. A new beau was beckoning. There was clearly no likelihood of a settled relationship between myself and her. Far better to leave it to chance to bring us together on some later date, as indeed it did. Moreover, I had two days earlier received some irritating news about my publishing situation in London. I will not bore the reader by explaining it in detail; confusion had arisen through my having delivered two manuscripts within three months of one another. It was not a desperate or indeed an immediate crisis, but I felt I would be more at peace if I talked it over with Peters and with Cassell's. Why not go back to London? I should not be at ease with Mary on the other side of the harbour; at any moment I might run into her at one of the parties along the coast or in a Nice or Antibes bistro. The difficulties with Cassell's provided me with an appropriate alibi. I should not appear to be behaving like an army in retreat, throwing away its packs and rifles. Exactly two weeks after I had been met at Nice by Mary, I caught a night train back to London.

Evelyn's *Scoop* was published in 1938. I wondered whether he had had Mary at all in mind, when he created the character of Kätchen. She has something of Mary's insouciance, amorality, friendliness, sense of a good time, a basic incapacity to come to terms with the 'establishment'. I reread it before I wrote this section. The resemblance did not seem so strong. But he may well have thought of her; most of his characters are blendings. Basil Seal in so many ways the late Peter Rodd was in many ways Evelyn himself. Evelyn did not see very much of Mary at the Welcome; he saw even less of Binks. Yet Binks, who was to achieve a very respected position as a painter, told me many years later that it was a conversation he had had with Evelyn that started his own conversion to Roman Catholicism. I was also reminded of Mary by Isherwood's Sally Bowles and Truman Capote's Holly Golightly. She had great loyalty to her friends, and she kept her friends. She could say very cruel things. She was often in ill health and expressed herself in flashes of ill temper. At the Welcome on her last day when she was settling her account at the desk, I said something that annoyed her. She swung round and kicked me on the shin. She was wearing a sharp pointed heel. It was very painful. 'I hate you,' she said. 'I've slept with you, but I hated it.' We were to laugh over that incident in later days.

She had a good critical brain, and she was a perceptive critic. She was someone with whom one could discuss one's work. She was a help to Binks with his painting. In 1938 she married a Time-Life correspondent. She was creatively interested in his work. Her comments were always helpful. Her promiscuity rarely hurt anybody's feelings. She was funny about it. In the middle 50s when she had a house in Milbrook, she came up to New York for an amorous siesta. The man concerned asked her when she had made love last. 'At six thirty this morning,' she informed him. Her comment to me later was, 'He thought he was offering me a treat.'

She was as outspoken as any woman I have ever known. She was completely uninhibited about herself. In the same way that she had suddenly dug her nails into my palm she would make unexpected passes at men, and women. 'But Eddie Wasserman,' I expostulated, 'what could you see in him?' 'He had some lovely records,' she replied. After I had left for London she spent a night at the Villa Marina. I could understand her finding Eldred attractive. 'I liked his shoes,' she said. In that respect she was not unlike Moravia's *Woman of Rome* who said that a courtesan who knew her *métier* would search for one attractive feature in a man who was attracted to her, then concentrate on that. It might be the way he moved his hands. 'I love his hands; therefore I love him.' Mary was like that, except that she did not look for a special feature. But when she found one she was prepared to consider herself attracted. 'Of course I wanted to make love with him. He had lovely records.'

After her break with Binks she was on her own in New York, maintaining a very pleasant flat. She never seemed short of money. She had a succession of beaux. For a time she worked at Polly Adler's,* though worked is not the word. She was not short of money and whenever she had made some at Polly's she would take a couple of the girls up to Harlem and spend it on them. 'I couldn't keep her on,' said Polly, 'she was disrupting my entire business.'

Mary introduced me to Polly in 1934; by then the great days of the establishment had passed. When the stockmarket was booming and prohibition was in flower, the police could very easily be suborned. The right sum to the right man, and all was well. But in the bright brave days of the N.R.A. with Jimmie Walker no longer at the city's helm, people like Polly Adler had to walk warily. By 1936 she preferred to be known as Polly Davies, but even so it was a very cosy club when Mary took me there. It really was a club; there was no solicitation. You sat around; you danced; you ordered drinks; no pressure was put upon you if you did not want to play. You took leave of your hostess just as you would at a cocktail party, and at the door a tall handsome dark girl would hand you a bill. It was usually less than you expected. Finance was never mentioned. Single drinks were a dollar a piece. I once asked Polly if she had any champagne. She shook her head. 'No Alec, there's no need for *you* to start ordering champagne here.' If she knew the ship that you were sailing by, there would be an 'au-revoir' cable signed by her and the particular girl whom you had cherished. Every year there was a Christmas card, with a parrot perched upon a ring. During the war, in far-off Baghdad it was nostalgic but reassuring to get that card each January.

Alas, when I was back again in New York in September 1945, the club was closed, and Polly, who had given the right sum to the wrong man, had had to serve a six months' sentence. She was then in retirement in California, planning to write her memoirs and to enrol in a university where she could get the degree that would give her the hallmark of respectability.

* Polly Adler in the 20s and 30s was New York's most famous 'madame'. She told her own story in *A House Is Not A Home*.

I met her for the last time in December 1955 at the Madrid airport as I queued up for my luggage. It was by Spanish time after ten at night but for me it was several hours later for I had been flying from Baghdad and the clock had been going back. I heard a voice, hoarse, low, powerful but attractive, that was unmistakable. I turned and it was she: scarcely altered – small, dumpy, animated, dark. She can never have been pretty. She probably looked better at thirty-five than she had at seventeen. Cuddlesome is the word for her. We fell into each other's arms.

I was desperately tired. I was catching a plane to Tangier early the following morning. I was being checked into a hotel as Iberia's guest. I longed for sleep but I could not miss the opportunity that this meeting provided of a long talk with Polly. She too was catching a plane next morning, though she was bound for Paris. 'Are we staying at the same hotel?' I asked.

'I'm staying at the Wellington.'

'So am I. Let's dine together.'

I had eaten on the plane. I was not hungry, but I could not miss this chance, the first I had ever had of a real talk with Polly. In her club there was always general conversation, a constant coming and going. I happened to be there once when one of my publisher's editorial staff walked in. He was young debonair, handsome. After a little gossip, she remarked, 'Frankie, you are so good looking. I've always meant to have an affair with you myself. Once I had it all planned out and then just at the wrong moment, a group came in from a deb dance. I had to see that they were taken care of.' Frankie laughed. 'I know, Polly. It's just the same for me as a publisher, I never have a chance to read a book.' I had my chance at last. What an opportunity. A *diner à deux* with Polly Adler.

'Are you hungry?' I asked.

'Not very.'

'Then let's have champagne and caviar.'

'Swell. I've always wanted to have a real talk with you.'

But it was not about the Club that she wanted to talk. In the old days one of her great assets as a hostess was her capacity to keep the talk light and lecherous – no dirty stories, no four-letter words, but the creation of an atmosphere which would make you think of love-making as the most reasonable occupation for human beings – a decameron atmosphere. 'Women and wine should life employ: is there aught else on earth desirous?'

But that kind of talk belonged to the past. She now wanted to tell me about her courses at the university. It was the most wonderful mental therapy. She had come out of prison with her nerves shattered; her self confidence destroyed. She had not dared to face her friends, but when she had a degree at Berkeley, she could look the world in the face, proudly. She told me about the courses she was reading. She recited her marks and credits. She recounted her difficulties with a particular professor. I could not have been more bored. I longed for sleep. Under the best conditions I feel drowsy if anyone talks for a quarter of an hour. A short sermon is as much as I can take. Polly went on and on. My eyelids slid over my eyes. But I must keep on, I told myself. This can't keep on for ever. Sooner or later she must get back to the old days. Memories of Mr Benchley, that was what I was waiting for. If only I could resist my somnolence; what a rich reward would be mine for gathering; but no, it was no good. On and on she went. 'French is my weak subject,' she informed me. 'That must surprise you, surely.' I was past being surprised. I felt like a batsman playing out time at the end of a long day, watching the minute hand creep on. 'I'm Russian by birth, you know that of course. You've read my book.' On and on and on . . . Twelve, half-past twelve, one o'clock. The restaurant was empty now. All the other tables were laid for breakfast. She looked round her. 'I suppose we shouldn't keep them up any longer.'

'I guess we shouldn't.'

'It's been a wonderful evening, Alec dear.'

'A memorable evening,' in many ways, I added to myself.

A winter or two later I received a Christmas card showing Polly resplendent in cap and gown, her social therapy completed.

As often happens, the publishing crisis that had encouraged me to return to England, proved in fact not to be a crisis at all. Three minutes' talk with Peters and the thing was settled. I did not even need to go round to Cassell's. I found myself at a loose end, therefore. I had no writing plans. It was too late in the year to organise any cricket for myself. Moreover, the weather was appalling. On the Wednesday I had the pleasure of taking my father to Lord's for the start of the Middlesex v. Warwick match. It was the first time that we had sat together in the pavilion. It was a sunny day. We saw Killick make 206 and G. T. S. Stevens, who had been a friend of my father's when he was a Hampstead schoolboy, 107. The next day I went down to Broadstairs to stay with H. S. Mackintosh, who had recently become the father of a son – he already had two daughters. He was fulfilling the role of a Victorian paterfamilias, taking his family to the beach to paddle, he himself encased in a knee to elbow woollen bathing suit. Nothing would induce me fresh from the Côte d'Azur to inflict such a penance on myself. It was so cold, my father notes in his diary, that fires were lighted at Underhill. My father also notes that he read with much enjoyment the manuscript of Rupert Croft-Cooke's novel *The Cow Jumped Over the Moon*, which on his recommendation Chapman and Hall accepted; a quarter of a century later I was to see a great deal of Croft-Cooke in Tangier.

It rained steadily all the time I was in Broadstairs, but I had an enjoyable time, with two good friends, exchanging good talk and consuming much excellent wine and food. On my return to Underhill at the end of the week I took my mother to see Edgar Wallace's 'The Old Man' at the Golders Green Hippodrome. On the Saturday I took my father to Lords' to the first day of the Middlesex and Kent match. In the evening I dined with Marda Vanne, the South African actress.

Marda for six years had been one of my dearest friends, and the news of her death four years ago, though I had not seen her for several years – she had spent much time in South Africa – was a great blow to me. The world seems a different place with her no longer in it. It is hard to describe her. She was short, neat, blonde, practical: she had one of those featureless putty faces that respond to make up. She was constantly altering her appearance to suit her hairdo. When I met her first in 1925 it was Eton cropped with a curl plastered across her ear. She was an excellent actress who never had star treatment. She was usually cast in supporting roles, Mrs Davidson, the pastor's wife, in 'Rain' for instance. She herself when I first knew her – she was then twenty-six – thought that she should act comedy, Marie Tempest parts – she had a look of Marie Tempest. But I think she lacked sex-appeal, on the stage. She lacked lightness. She did not look embraceable. Moreover she had a deep nature. I pictured her in more emotional roles, as a mature woman. Though she was not indifferent to men, she was married to a prominent South African politician, and had several love affairs which the men involved found satisfactory, she was mainly interested in women. I thought she might in her forties and fifties find emotional release in the roles of aunts, mothers, schoolmistresses who could be legitimately involved with younger women. But when her forties came, she went back to South Africa for the war. She did return on occasions to England afterwards, but I do not remember seeing her in an important part. During the war she was active in the South African theatre.

On that August evening we dined at the R.A.C. It seems a curious place to which to take an actress but the Savile was closed for the staff's summer holiday. We were temporary members of the R.A.C., and I thought the gilt and marble, the height and width of its main dining-room would be a contrast to the speak-easies of Manhattan, and the Mediterranean bistros with which I had become over-familiar during the last ten months. We dined rather well indeed, had a refreshing bottle of champagne and danced to a reasonable band. 'I mustn't stay up too late,' Marda said. 'Gwen and I are going to Cornwall tomorrow.'

Gwen was Gwen Françgon Davies who had recently starred in *The Barretts of Wimpole Street* and with whom Marda for several years had shared a house. They were motoring down, she told me, starting next morning at eight o'clock. They were stopping the night near Exeter, in a hotel at Chagford; they were aiming to spend a week or two in Cornwall at Mousehole, a fishing village near Newlyn which had been for many years a favourite haunt of painters. 'I envy you,' I said.

'Why don't you come along with us? There's a seat in the car.'

'Why don't I.'

It was arranged like that, within five minutes. When my parents came down next morning, for their cup of tea before early service, they found me in a country suit, with a suitcase packed.

This trip was to have historic consequences. It started the boom of the Easton Court Hotel, which was through the next twenty-five years to fill a footnote in literary memories.

Marda Vanne had heard of it from the South African painter Edward Wolfe, who had a house in Tangier. Wolfe had made friends there with a youngish Englishman called Norman Webb who was employed by some charitable organisation for the benefit of African animals. His organisation was based on Fez. To Fez had come on a holiday a middle-aged American divorcée called Mrs Posthelthwaite Cobb. She was a member of seaboard society; at a loose end, with her two children married and no base in the United States, she formed an attachment for Norman Webb. It seemed to her that he was being wasted in Morocco, as indeed he was. It was a dead-end occupation. She had means. She wanted to do something for him. She also wanted, it may be presumed, to give some base of security to their relationship. Marriage would have been inappropriate; moreover marriage would have given Norman rights over her that she was not anxious to concede. Why not a business partnership? Why not a hotel in England? That was how the Easton Court Hotel came into being.

Edward Wolfe, a South African, and a life-long friend of Marda, had told her about this venture. 'Go down and have a look at it,' he urged her. As it made a useful halfway halt on the way to Cornwall, she decided to follow his advice.

We arrived there in the late afternoon. A grey rain-cluttered day was ending in a sunset that promised better things for the next morning. Easton Court lay two miles north of Chagford. It consisted at that time of a single two-storied fourteenth-century farm house. Its rooms were low and dark, with small windows and open beams. It was built of stone, and thatched. It had an uneven staircase. It lay on the highroad to Okehampton, but a high thick stone wall protected it from the noise of traffic. It was furnished with cottage-style antiques, coffin stools and Staffordshire figures – that kind of thing. A notice recorded that the antiques were for sale. On the walls were a number of Edward Wolfe's Moroccan pictures.

At the Easton Court there was an attractive maid; dark, plump vivacious. I had taken no particular note of her, perhaps because she had taken no particular note of me. But she had taken note of Marda's chauffeur. He was young, vigorous and handsome, but what had especially attracted her was his chauffeur's cap. She had a *faiblesse* for 'men in uniform' and the chauffeur left the hotel resolved that on our return journey we should stop there so that he could further exploit that weakness.

We planned to spend three weeks at Mousehole in a pub of which we were the only guests. We had a sitting room at our disposal. On the ground floor was a tap room where we could challenge the fishermen to games of darts and dominoes. Marda and Gwen had friends in the neighbourhood – Laura and Harold Knight who had studios and a house there. Sir Barry Jackson was across the way in Newlyn. Scott Sunderland was his house guest. Sunderland had acted the part of Robert Browning in 'The Barretts of Wimpole Street'. It was a perfect piece of casting. He was tall, strong, handsome, athletic. He exuded health. Yet he was in fact a complete hypochondriac. He was always fussing about his health. His dressing-room cupboard was filled with bottles and pills. He was for ever taking a new cure for some imagined ailment; spiritually and mentally no one could have been less like Robert Browning.

I heard much good theatre talk. Gwen told me that acting with Cedric Hardwicke was a curious experience. After a play had been running for three weeks, he became a zombie. He went through his part perfectly, without knowing what he was doing. It was disconcerting, she said, to be seated on a sofa beside a man who was making you a declaration of passionate devotion, when you could tell from his eyes that he was not there at all. The reader may remember that one of the most telling scenes in the play was an expression of paternal love. When the cast was rehearsing the play, they always referred to it as 'the incest scene'. It was then learnt that the Barrett family was meditating an injunction and a libel action against the play, and the cast was solemnly adjured

143

that never, never anywhere were they in future to mention the word 'incest'. The play incidentally never mentioned what may have been one of Barrett's strongest objections to Browning as his daughter's husband. The Barretts came from Jamaica from the white planter aristocracy. Browning came from St Kitts and very certainly had coloured blood. He was sometimes mistaken for an Italian.

The rain during our visit to Mousehole fell continuously, but a fishing port does not lose its charm when it is raining. Fishing smacks are just as busy in bad weather. Mousehole was supported by its pilchard trade with Italy. I had not eaten pilchards until the war, when they came up in rations, in tins flooded in tomato sauce; the men found them 'tasty'. After the war they vanished from the market. At our hotel they were served fresh for breakfast and were excellent.

Our plan to spend three weeks in Mousehole was disturbed by Marda's sudden recall to London for rehearsals. Gwen and I decided to motor home by slow stages. It was then that the chauffeur's need to return to Easton Court became insistent. There was no point in making a succession of short trips; one saw nothing that way, he argued. One was always packing and unpacking. Far better to operate from a central base: making daily excursions to various beauty spots. What better base could we have than Easton Court?

If one person in a party has a definite objective, he usually gets his way. Gwen and I did not care very much what we did. She needed to be back by a certain date and that was all. I had no obligations. I could take my time. What not Easton Court? I was the readier to fall in with a plan that saved me constant packing and unpacking, because I had just been inveigled into a writing project that would keep me busy for three weeks. The project was not in itself an important one, but in retrospect it can be seen as the start of the greatest of all changes in publishing, the paperback.

Sir Allen Lane started Penguins in 1936, but the idea of a small paper-bound book that would fit the pocket came from Sir Ernest Benn. His idea was not for a reprint but for a new story. I was one of the authors approached. The fee offered was £200 on account of a small royalty. £200 was to me a useful amount of money, and I had available a serial story that had come out in the *Daily Mirror* twenty months before. I had not thought it good enough to publish in hard cover and present to the critics and the public as a serious contribution to the Alec Waugh Oeuvre, if such a thing existed, but it could, I felt, be cut and doctored into a reasonably presentable thirty thousand word *novella*.

The story was called 'Leap Before You Look'. It opened with a young couple, very much in love but with the young man postponing marriage until his career can be adequately launched. The girl in pique marries another man. It was a typical magazine short story, told with magazine adroitness. The reader became interested in the couple, was anxious to know what happened to them, and was ready to follow their fortunes through a series of improbably melodramatic situations that included a revolution in a West Indian republic. It was a readable piece of merchandise, and when Farrar and Rinehart in the summer of 1930 decided to issue a series of dollar books and asked their authors if they had not some neglected manuscript that they could include as they needed to get the books upon the market quickly, I gave them *Leap Before You Look*. The series failed before my book was published, but as the book had been set up in type they decided to issue it as an ordinary $2.50 novel. It came out in 1933. It was not extensively reviewed. It did not sell very many copies, but I am not aware that it did me any harm, and I had some fun with the five hundred dollars that it earned me.

The book has had in fact a curious subterranean existence. In 1935 when Cassell's issued a series of hardback novels at 3s. 6d., it was included in it, and in the early days of paperbacks, before and during the second war, it was twice included in minor collections of popular fiction. As late as 1950 an offer was made for it by one of the better London houses. But this I refused. If too many copies of it were in circulation, there was a danger of my being judged by it rather than by one of the novels into which I have put more of myself: the moral of the episode is, I suppose, that if you can really interest a reader in characters and a situation in the early pages you will make him read on until the end. Many excellent novels do not grip the reader's interest until the hundredth page.

Benn's 9d. novels were a failure. They were extensively publicised, with whole page advertisements and a large lunch (which I was unable to attend) for the launching of the first six volumes. But the public did not respond. I fancy because the books were not good enough. The thirty thousand-word *novella* is an admirable medium. It can be read in a couple of sittings, its impact is concentrated. But there are very few good *novellas* in the English language. Maugham's stories are a lot shorter. It is a length for which there is no obvious market, and few writers will set to work on something that there is little hope of selling, so that an English writer who has an idea that could make a *novella* would prefer to enlarge it to novel length and make a reasonable sum of money. I suspect that most of the contributors to the series did as I did and hashed up something that lay idle in a desk. The only contribution that seemed to me a genuinely chosen subject was G. B. Stern's *Long Lost Father*.

For me the significance of this commission to contribute to the series was that it decided me to write the book at Easton Court after Gwen Frangçon Davies had returned to London. By staying there two weeks I came to appreciate the charms of that part of Devonshire, and also the charms of the hotel itself. Working quietly upon the story – it was mainly a job of scissors and paste – I failed to appreciate the significance of the political news that was filling the columns of the Newspapers. There had been so many scares about the country's tottering economy, so many cries of 'Wolf, Wolf', that I suspected, as nearly all the papers were owned by the Tories, that these alarmist reports were part of a Tory attack upon the Labour government.

I was more interested in the publication of my father's autobiography, and in the gloom that was harassing Chapman and Hall's activities. They had found that already the sales for 1931 were down by three thousand pounds. On the other hand the auguries for *One Man's Road* were good. Hugh Walpole and J. B. Priestly liked it, and it was due for a Book Society recommendation. It was to be published in the same week as Ernest Rhys' autobiography *Everyman Remembers*. The two books were certain to be reviewed together. My father did not consider this a disadvantage. He and Rhys were old friends; there could be no question of jealousy between them. And the two books were so different that they would provide the reviewer with useful comparisons. Rhys' book was very largely about the people whom he had met. It was anecdotal. My father's was a personal, subjective narrative. My father expected that *Everyman Remembers* would sell better than *The Road*. I do not know whether it did, but the sales of *The Road* were highly satisfactory. Chapman and Hall's traveller said that he did not expect to subscribe more than 300 copies, but actually the subscription order was 403 and my father's diary contains weekly references to repeat orders. In its first week 164 copies were sold. In the next week 170. In the fourth 82. The reviews, with the exception of *The Times Literary Supplement*, were excellent. Many old friends wrote to express their delight with it. It was the kind of book that invited correspondence. Contemporaries wrote to exchange points of view. It made a happy September for my father. So was it a happy month for Evelyn who was back now from his idyll in the South of France with the first ten thousand words of a new novel. It was then called *Accession* and my father found it excellent. It was to appear a year later as *Black Mischief*.

XI

The best account of the financial crisis that I have read is Harold Nicolson's in his life of King George V. Harold Nicolson was Sir Oswald Mosley's associate in the launching of the New Party, and his diaries of 1931 provide a day to day record of what was happening behind the scenes. The crisis was precipitated in the middle of June by the failure of the *Credit Anstalt* of Vienna. In the same month the Committee of Finance and Industry presented its report of which Philip Snowdon, the Chancellor of the Exchequer stated in the House of Commons that the economies recommended were so fierce that the house must be united. *Punch* on August the 5th had a cartoon called 'The Half Nelson Touch', showing the report of the Economical Committee presented as a snake, with Snowdon looking at it through the wrong end of the telescope. The caption ran, 'It all depends on how you look at these things; as I see it, it seems quite insignificant'.

By the middle of August it had become plain that the Bank of England could not support the pound without loans from New York and Paris, whose bankers were refusing to make loans until Britain could present a balanced budget; this would involve a heavy cut in government expenditure: in particular a cutting of the unemployment benefit – 'the dole' – which was an essential part of the Labour programme. It was unlikely that the Trades Union Congress would agree to that. The Prime Minister, Ramsay Macdonald, cut short his holiday in Scotland and returned to London. So did Baldwin, who was in Aix-les-Bains. There was a succession of consultations between the party leaders. It was clear that the crisis had become a national issue, with all the parties agreeing on a policy. *Punch* had a cartoon of Macdonald preparing to cut down the tree of national extravagance and Baldwin and Sir Herbert Samuel, the leader of the Liberal Party, saying, 'Look here if you really mean to use that axe, we'll bury the hatchet'.

The problem was, however, to get the Labour Party to agree. Meeting followed meeting. Baldwin returned to Aix-les-Bains. The T.U.C. refused to commit itself until its meeting early in September. The rain fell steadily. On the 21st first class cricket was only possible in three matches. On August the 24th the King on his own initiative came up from Scotland. As Harold Nicolson points out, he never went beyond his constitutional powers, but his part was a decisive one. Baldwin too, returned to London and the King saw both him and Samuel. Macdonald continued to argue with his cabinet. He could not get them to agree to the economies that would allow the budget to be balanced. He had no alternative, he said, to resignation. He went to Buckingham Palace to resign. But to the astonishment of his cabinet he returned with the announcement that the King had refused to accept his resignation, and that he had agreed himself without committing his colleagues, to lead a national government in company with Baldwin's Conservatives and Samuel's Liberals, for the length of the emergency.

At first there was pandemonium in the Cabinet Room. Then when order was re-established, Herbert Morrison, one of the youngest members, was the first to speak. 'Well, Prime Minister, it is very easy to get into such a combination! You will find it very difficult to get out of it and I, for one, am not coming with you'. Only J. H. Thomas and Philip Snowdon – and he with considerable reluctance – joined Macdonald. The mass of the party never forgave him. They felt that he had betrayed them, that the whole thing was a 'banker's ramp'.

Not surprisingly, since the National Government handed over control to the Tories – and the Press was mainly owned by the Tories – the change over was welcomed enthusiastically in Fleet Street. *Punch* had a cartoon of Ramsay Macdonald, Baldwin and Samuel pulling on a rope, under the eyes of Mr Punch, with the caption, 'and a pull altogether or so Mr Punch hopes'. On September 2 the pound was presented on a tight rope marked 'financial crisis' with the caption, 'the eyes of the world are upon me, and I'm not going to lose my balance'. Macdonald and the T.U.C. were shown in conflict as Roman warriors. There was an air of facile optimism. The clauses of the Economy Budget were announced. The basic rate of Income Tax was raised from 4s 6d to 5s. Ministerial salaries of over five thousand pounds were cut by twenty per cent; of over two thousand pounds by fifteen per cent; ten per cent on lower salaries. Judges' and teachers' salaries were down: the dole was cut, and there was a reduction in pay and pensions for defence services. *Punch*'s cartoon showed John Bull pushing a barrow piled with higher duties and more taxes, with the caption 'well, here goes, the hard road to safety'.

I do not remember that I or any of my friends were particularly agitated about all this. We were none of us salaried civil servants. Few of us had property. Our incomes were small and fluctuant. We lived from hand to mouth, from article to article. At the start of a year we could only guess at what we should earn; we would have lucky and unlucky breaks – as a golfer has; one day his putts drop, the next day they don't. My father's diary contains no references to the forming of the National Government, nor does my mother's.

By the middle of the third week in September, I had finished my adaptation of *Leap Before You Look*. There seemed no point in my staying on at Chagford any longer. I decided to return to London, pausing to visit my uncle George Raban, the Vicar of Bishop's Hull, a small village two and half miles from Taunton. I had no plans beyond that. I might go down to the South of France. Mary was in Paris. I might pause on the way to see her. It might be a good idea to meet her in a different setting. The great advantage of being a freelance was that I had not to make plans in advance. All seemed for the best in the best of all possible worlds. And then out of the blue, an event occurred of whose significance I was unaware because it was deliberately played down in the British Press and I am a casual reader. On Thursday, September 17, the British North Atlantic fleet in Invergorden mutinied because of the pay cuts, and Wall Street and the Continent of Europe, where the incident was prominently reported, became convinced that Britain was on the verge of anarchy. All hands to the pumps if there were any pumps to man.

Later, the Opposition was to say, 'at Jutland in 1916 the British

Navy beat the ex-Kaiser – at Invergorden in 1931, it beat Mr Montagu Norman and the Bank of England.'

On Saturday, September the 19th a young American student in Edinburgh went to his bank to cash a large book of travellers cheques. He had come to the conclusion that he could not afford the extra year at the university that he would have liked. He had better draw out what money he had left, take a short holiday, and return to the United States. The cashier looked at the travellers cheques, then looked at the young man. 'May I give you some advice,' he said. 'May I suggest that you cash these cheques on Monday morning. It will be a convenience for us both.'

On Sunday the National Government which had assumed power in order to protect the pound decided to leave the Gold Standard. On the Monday morning, the American student's travellers cheques were worth so much more that their owner felt he would be justified in staying an extra year in the university. The student's name was James Michener. Seventeen years later his opera *South Pacific* was an international moneymagnet. How much did that bank teller's advice affect his future? Who can tell? The course of his career might have been very different.

For me, as I suppose for most Britons born before 1910, the announcement on that Monday morning was the biggest shock that we had known or were to know. Other shocks, such as the declarations of wars, the overthrowing of presidents and princes, the outburst of revolutions, were things that had been foreseen or were happening somewhere else. They had not given one the feeling that 'the pillared firmament was rottenness and earth's base built on stubble'.

'Safe as the Rock of Gibraltar,' 'Safe as the Bank of England', these had been the 'two main pillars vaulted high' that sustained our way of life. From one point of view it made no difference to me at all. I had no investments whose value had been cut in half; on the contrary the dollars that were due to me from New York would now have a greater purchasing power in England. It was not a personal, it was a national disaster. Sitting on the lawn of the hotel, in the bland autumn sunlight, I read first the headlines, then the first leader, then the various news items.

The Times was urbanely reassuring. 'There is,' it said, 'no cause for alarm in the decision which the Government has reached. On the contrary its action will inure to the benefit not only of this country but also of the whole world.'

That night on the wireless Philip Snowdown spoke as a bitterly disappointed but still spirited man. The crisis had been intensified by false pessimism. There had been no united front, then there had been the unrest in the Navy. He adjured his fellow countrymen to keep their heads.

Myself, I was impatient to get back to London, to find out what was really happening, to sit in the sand parlour at the Savile and hear what the men who were behind the news were thinking. I regretted the two days I had to spend at Bishop's Hull.

On the third morning after England had left the Gold Standard, I found him in high spirits. 'This is exactly what the country needs,' he said. 'We have been idle, living on the past. We must recognise that the world is changing. This is the challenge that we as a country needed.' My Uncle George was dependent entirely on his stipend as a Parish priest and on the interest on his not very large investments. If the pound were to collapse in the way that the mark and franc had done, he would be in a bad position, but he was not worrying about himself. He saw the government's failure as the spur the country needed. 'That is what I am going to say on Sunday in my evening sermon. The Government is we ourselves. It is because we, as individuals have been living selfishly and imprudently, that we are in trouble.' He paused, then he gave one of the little giggles that made people wonder if he was 'all there', 'I must inspire my flock, Alec, inspire my flock.'

Was England as a whole going to accept the fallibility of the Bank of England as a spur to effort? If it was, then indeed the devaluation of our currency might prove to be the spur we needed. It was from my Uncle George that I got the first clue to what the national temper was to be during the autumn that lay ahead.

The two days I spent at Bishop's Hull were a pleasant breathing space before the necessary making of decisions that awaited me in

London. It was twenty years since I had been there. But up till my grandfather's death in 1912, we went there every summer. My parents took a holiday abroad at the end of July, then they would divide two weeks between my father's family at Midsomer Norton and my mother's here at Bishop's Hull. At Midsomer Norton there was a local family that organised boys' cricket games. At Bishop's Hull I used to watch Somerset play at Taunton. The two holidays complemented one another. I looked forward to each equally. There was only one feature of the holiday to which I did not look forward, that was the harvester bugs that in Bishop's Hull used to attack my head, and raise welts in my hair. I wondered if they would be as voracious still. To my relief they were not. Perhaps the last week in September was too late for them. Perhaps they found my bald scalp unappetizing. At any rate I slept at peace.

They were the last nights I was to spend there; I only once came again to Bishop's Hull for my Aunt Mildred's funeral, my Uncle George having shortly after the war moved to another parish. If I had known it was to be my last visit I would have taken a more nostalgic inventory of the pictures, the furniture, the decorations I should never see again.

It all looked very much as it had in 1911, that miraculously long hot summer when Middlesex so nearly won the county championship. There had been a great deal of building in the neighbourhood, and there was a succession of small houses along the road out from Taunton, but the field that lay opposite the vicarage garden was still used agriculturally, so that looking from my bedroom I had a sense of being in the open country, in the big house of a considerable estate. There was no longer a gardener, just a boy who came in two days a week; the greenhouses were no longer used, weeds grew in the paths, and the two thatched summerhouses that had served as forts during my days of childhood make-believe had slid into collapse. In my grandfather's day the lawn had been used for both tennis and croquet, and in the porch there were a couple of targets which had been set up for archery. It was many years since there had been any parties or games at Bishop's Hull. Yet my uncle and aunts had a horror of throwing anything away. When they eventually moved to another vicarage they took with them the rotting targets, the croquet hoops and mallets, and stringless tennis racquets. They also took with them all the old clothes that my grandmother had worn in Delhi in the 1850s, including the air cushions which she had placed in her carriage when she was pregnant, and of which the rubber had long since perished. My grandmother's second husband had been quite well to do, but they had been an improvident couple, pennywise and pound foolish, and they did not leave a great deal to their children. Perhaps it was because of this that my aunts and uncle were so anxious to hold on to all the relics of their former affluence. I was grateful to them for this. My childhood was very real to me as I spent those two days surrounded by objects that recalled it.

The youthful student of history is led to believe that the happiness of the individual depends on the rise and fall of his country's fortunes; that an English family must have been exuberant in 1588 after the defeat of the Armada, and bowed in gloom in 1782 after the loss of the thirteen colonies. But that is not invariably the case. One's own fortunes do not run parallel with one's country's – certainly they did not in the case of my old friend A. D. Peters. I had arranged to have dinner with him on my first Saturday in London at the Savile Club, of which we were both members. I had imagined that we should have a long and serious talk about the effect that the gold standard crisis would have upon the literary market. Not at all.

'What are your immediate plans?' he asked.

'I was thinking of trying some short stories.'

'I didn't mean that. Are you coming back to London?'

I shook my head. The one evening that I had spent at Underhill had warned me that London would be restless during the next two weeks. There was certain to be a general election shortly and till that was over, social life in London would be disorganised. A week earlier I had been planning a return to Villefranche. But that was now impossible, not only, or indeed not mainly because the value of the pound abroad was so uncertain but because a

Briton saw it as his duty not to go abroad unless he had an essential reason. We had been trusted to 'Buy British' and not to take sterling out of the country. Buy British. South African wine instead of French. I could see no alternative to a return to Chagford. I explained this to Peters. 'In that case, you won't need your flat', he said. 'Will you let me use it?'

'What on earth for?'

'I've left Helen.'

It was a complete surprise to me. I had thought that they were an ideally happy couple.

'Is there somebody else?' I asked.

'Yes, but she's not the reason. How soon can I have your flat?'

'As soon as you like.'

His need of my flat hastened my return to Chagford. There was no reason for me to stay in London, spending money needlessly. I stayed for a few days at Underhill. I took my mother to see 'Victoria and her Hussar' and 'The Ringer' which was on at the Golders Green Hippodrome. On the Friday I took my father to a morning showing of a film in London. We lunched at the Savile, where we met A. D. Peters and Earle Welby, then I caught the three thirty from Waterloo to Exeter.

Norman Webb was there to meet me. 'You're a pint and a half late,' he said. He always judged the lateness of a train by the amount of beer that he could consume while he was waiting for it.

My return to Chagford was symbolic of the country's temper; the English were coming home to man their defences, in the face of the foe. My Uncle George's prophecy had proved correct. The Duke of Connaught, who had a villa in Cap Ferrat, announced that he would spend the winter in Sidmouth. Later in the year he was interviewed on a news film, strolling along the waterfront, wrapped in a heavy coat. There was a palm tree in the background.

One by one the semi-expatriates who had spent their Augusts stretched on beaches in the sun, returned each with his own story of the difficulties he had had in raising the fare home. How the French had enjoyed pretending that the pound was valueless!

Patrick Balfour was one of them. I had written to him in August telling him of my discovery of Easton Court. He now asked me to book a room for him. His return was a great piece of good fortune for the hotel. Patrick was in a difficult position. He had just, but only just, enough money to finance a winter in the South of France, staying with friends and in small hotels. But he could not afford to live in London. The rent from his flat was one of his few assets. He had to find in England some equivalent for Villefranche – a place where he could live cheaply and work. Liking Easton Court at sight, he decided to make it his winter base.

He was and is a very social person. He needed a place not only where he could write but where he could see his friends. Easton Court answered all his problems. He wrote round to his friends, urging them to visit him. He was popular and his appeals were answered. During that autumn the hotel was visited by Alan Pryce-Jones, John Collier, Helen Kapp, Piers Synott, Christopher Hobhouse, Godfrey Winn, Edward Sackville West. My brother Evelyn paid his first visit in November. Thanks to Patrick there was a steady stream of guests, and what is more important precisely the kind of guest that the hotel wanted – members of the same group of artistic bohemians who knew each other and knew about each other. A visitor would have got the impression that they were guests in a country house. Patrick publicised their visits. Within six months, the hotel was an established locality in gossip columns, and Mrs Cobb was able with a clear conscience to order architects and builders to erect behind the original farmhouse an L-shaped modern two-storied wing, with central heating, invisible from the road, that would accommodate a dozen guests.

The hotel was to flourish for a quarter of a century and the pattern of its life was set during that first autumn. A licence to serve alcohol was never acquired, and Mrs Cobb was wise in not pressing for one. It would have ruined the special atmosphere. Motorists would have started dropping in. At Moreton-Hampstead there was a big hotel, a converted private house, owned by the Southern Railway. Bright young people on a golfing holiday might well have said to one another after dinner, 'I hear that there are always some amusing young women at the Easton Court. Let's test the rumour.' Mrs Cobb was anxious to preserve her privacy. Her guests could drink hard liquor in their rooms; they could have wine or beer upon their tables. After dinner they could, if they wished, drive out to one of the local inns and drink beer in the taproom. She herself organised a cocktail session in her own room every evening.

She lived in conditions that would have astonished her fellow members of seaboard society. Her whole life was conducted in a single room on the ground floor of what had presumably once been a stables. It was not a very large room. It contained a large double bed, and a few chairs. In the bay window was a table and during the day the space occupied by the bay window was the hotel's office. Beside the fireplace was a dog basket, that was filled at night by a small malodorous dog called 'Nannie'. The hotel's telegraphic address was 'Nannie'. Opening off the bedroom was a narrow passage where a curtain concealed a succession of coat-hangers. At the end of the passage was the bathroom and the toilet. The passage was littered with indiscriminate articles; there was a cooking stove; a table for preparing drinks; there was a number of full and emptying bottles. Nothing could have been further removed from the style in which her children lived. Here every evening her closer friends among the guests would assemble for a preprandial sundowner. In that first autumn we concentrated upon a concoction of Canadian Club Whisky and pure fruit juice, in equal proportions, with the fruit juice consisting of three-quarters orange juice and one quarter lemon. A teaspoonful of sugar was added. It was iced and stirred, not shaken.

The evening cocktail was an amenity greatly appreciated by the female guests. It was not unusual for young men to arrive accompanied by females. Mrs Cobb maintained appearances, and would not allow unmarried couples to share a room, but she put herself out to make unofficial ladies feel at home. In those days – this happened after all forty years ago – young women were often chary of accompanying young men on trips, because they did not like 'the way the servants looked at them'. Mrs Cobb made them feel respectable and respected.

It is not easy to describe Caroline Cobb. She was short and

dumpy. She was a ramshackle kind of woman, but to present her as resembling one of Helen Hokinson's club women, would be to leave out her sense of humour. She could be very funny. She was excellent company. Yet she did not indulge in monologues. She encouraged good talk in others. She liked bohemians, and in particular welcomed writers. Several of the bedrooms were furnished with small refectory tables, which served admirably as desks. Most writers like to spread their papers round them and, later, Mrs Cobb was to advertise the hotel in the P.E.N. Club news as 'understanding writers' ways' and 'providing stout tables'.

Within a year the hotel had become well known in the world of authorship, and the 'Cobbwebbs' became familiar figures in London parties. In June 1940 when France fell and a special ship was sent to take Americans home, although her family and friends urged her to return, Caroline stood her ground, courageously but wisely. 'What would I do in New York,' she asked, 'sit around over martinis in the Colony?' But that was said for effect. That was not the real reason. During her ten years she had become identified with England's interests. If the country was to be invaded, she preferred to share the adversities as she had shared the good times of the English. To run a hotel in the country, was her contribution to the war effort. And a very valuable contribution it was too. Many of us took our leaves there, and Evelyn – convalescent after an accident – went there to write *Brideshead Revisited*. In war time, as in peace time, Easton Court played an important role in the lives of many of us. After the war the tradition was maintained. Its stout tables continued to support the manuscripts of, among many others, Patrick Leigh Fermour, Louise Brogan, C. P. Snow and Pamela Hansford Johnson. It has figured and will figure in many memoirs.

It was England's devaluation of the pound, and Patrick Balfour's need of a quiet base in the country that got it started. But unless that pretty housemaid's interest had been woken by a chauffeur's cap, Patrick Balfour would not have ever heard of it.

XII

My father's diary records against October 9 'weather improved,' and it was a singularly lovely autumn. Morning after morning a red gold sun shone on to a lawn glistening with dew and mist. It was so warm that I could sit in the garden working. The sky was blue: with an occasional dove-coloured cloud drifting slowly over it. Beside the wall flanking a Tudor gateway ran a bed of chrysanthemums dotted with a few late roses. It was six years since I had spent an autumn in England, in the country. During those years I had seen much beauty: the palm trees of the Pacific, the blue mountains of New South Wales, the brown rivers of Malaya; but the rounded, varied, many-coloured beauty of north Devon had a softer, deeper, tenderer appeal.

There were stables close to the hotel. Most afternoons I rode for a couple of hours through high-hedged lanes looking down over the low rounded hills, across patterned valleys to the smoke of villages: thatched roofs; square-spired churches. Very calm it was and peaceful. It was hard to believe that its security was menaced; that English people would not live here dreamily in peace for centuries, as they had for centuries.

Most evenings I stopped for a glass of cider at the Ring of Bells in North Bovey; letting my horse graze upon the green. North Bovey is a very lovely village. Thatched, low-built, white-washed, it is built on a slope and in a circle. The Ring of Bells is set back a little. Seated in its porch, you see, framed in the oblong gap between two white walls, through the wide-spread boughs of an oak tree, the outline of the church, and the gilt hands of its clock. The inn-keeper then was a little old woman close on eighty, grey-haired and wrinkled, and a spinster. She wore a long, black silk dress with a miniature set as a brooch in its high-boned collar. The house had been in her family for three generations. Farm-hands and an occasional groom came to sit beside me in the porch. We would chatter casually of football and the weather. Dusk would be falling when I left. The horse with its nose set for home would canter back through the narrow lanes. Low mists drifted along the hills. Lights showed in the valleys. The far purple of Dartmoor deepened into black.

During the mornings I worked on a series of short stories. None of them came to much. There were then so many magazines in England that a story had to be very bad, or very, very good not to find a purchaser; and all of these stories were sold eventually in England, but Carl Brandt had no illusions about them. They were not worth sending out, he said. The American market was very difficult and if I wanted to break into it, I should have to work a great deal harder. Which was of course perfectly true. I was very casual with those short stories. I did not live with them before I wrote them. I was enjoying myself too much, in lively company. Moreover there was the hourly excitement of public events.

The General Election was fixed for October 27. Every day brought fresh evidence of the energy with which the country was settling down to its huge task of restoration. I wrote those stories with a minute part of myself. One of the stories has an interest, however, apart from any quality it possessed. I had the idea of a perfect murder. Two strangers meet in a pub; they each admit that their lives are ruined by the existence of one single person in their life. In the case of one man it is a wife. In the case of the other, it is an aunt from whom he will inherit a fortune. If that one person were to die then the world would be cloudless. 'If I were to murder my wife,' says the one, 'I should certainly be discovered. I am the one person who would profit. They would check my movements. I could have no alibi.'

'I am in exactly the same position,' says the other. 'If my aunt were to die, I should be suspect from the start.' He pauses. 'But if I were to murder your wife, no one would suspect me. Why should anyone connect me with your wife, and you would have a cast-iron alibi.'

'In the same way I could murder your aunt with impunity.' They agree to perform each his own murder for the other.

As far as I know, the idea was my own completely. I made a twelve hundred word short story out of the idea and sold it to the

Evening News for seven guineas. Twenty years later I saw a film 'Strangers on a Train' based on a novel by Patricia Highsmith, that was constructed on the same idea. In 1958 Nicholas Blake published a novel called *A Penknife In My Heart*. The postscript said, 'After this book had gone to press, I discovered that the basis of its plot is similar to that of a novel by Patricia Highsmith, *Strangers on a Train* published in 1950 by the Cresset Press and made into a film. I had never read this novel or seen the film nor do I remember hearing about them.'

It is very easy for two writers to get the same idea simultaneously. In 1953–4 Nicholas Montserrat, whom I have never met, was at work in South Africa on a novel very similar to the one on which I was at work in the South of France. The main plot concerned a British colony in the tropics, that is afflicted by racial and political unrest. This unrest is accerbated by an unscrupulous journalist. Without his articles bloodshed could have been avoided, but because of them there is violence and sudden death. Montserrat set his story in Africa, I set mine in the West Indies. His was called *The Tribe That Lost Its Head*, mine, *Island in the Sun*. The various sub-plots were completely different, but the books were basically the same. They were both published in 1956 and made the best seller lists for about the same number of weeks.

Certain ideas are in the air, and different writers catch them independently; that is after all what timing is. The best example of this is the spate of warbooks that appeared in 1928–9, *All Quiet on the Western Front, Goodbye to All That, Her Privates We, Undertones of War, Death of a Hero, Memoirs of a Fox-Hunting Man*. No publisher, no press agent, could have foreseen this boom. Books of such quality could not have been written in a hurry to meet a sudden need. There was no question of Chatto & Windus ringing up Aldington and saying, 'There's a demand for war memoirs. Why not write us yours? The books, all of them, were quietly and deeply digested. During 1927 and early 1928 a number of ex-soldiers found themselves wanting to relive their war years. Immediately after the war, they had been abjured, 'nothing about the war. We all want to forget that.' But when a book insists upon getting written, it gets written. And the fact that in

1927 so many writers were feeling impelled to relive their war experiences, would have been an indication to anyone who had known they were – which no one could have known – that in a very short time their contemporaries would be wanting to read about the war, the writer being usually ahead of his time. H. G. Wells said that timeliness was the secret of best-sellerdom. It is not that a novelist writes what he thinks the public wants to read; but that he is impelled to write about what the public will be wanting to read shortly. Being in tune with one's time is being ahead of one's time, but not too far ahead of it; the public will be able to catch up with you.

A classic example of timeliness was provided that very autumn by Noël Coward's play 'Cavalcade'. In his autobiography *Present Indicative* he has described how in the autumn of 1930 while he was acting in 'Private Lives', he got the idea for a spectacular production at the Coliseum. He planned to start it with scenes from the Second Empire. Then in Foyle's book shop he found some bound volumes of *Black and White* and the *Illustrated London News*. In the first volume was a full-page picture of a troop-ship leaving for the Boer War. He recalled the tunes of the hour – Dolly Grey, Blue Bell, Soldiers of the Queen. In a flash – it was 'sheer luck' he said – the full and changed idea came to him. England from New Year's Eve 1899 to New Year's Eve 1930. He sought the advice of G. B. Stern who, being several years older than himself had a more vivid memory of the Boer War atmosphere, and to whom he dedicated the published play. He visualised a play, threaded on a string of the popular songs, and a woman somewhat like his own mother and . . . and this was the key point – like a million others – 'ordinary, kind and unobtrusively brave, capable of deep suffering and incapable of cheap complaint.' Into this woman's mouth he was to put the final curtain speech that would express the beliefs and faith of the millions like herself, a speech that is now part of the theatre's heritage:

Let's couple the future of England with the past of England; the glories and victories that are over, and the sorrows that are over too. Let's drink to our sons who made part of the pattern, and to our hearts that died with them. Let's drink to the spirit of gallantry and courage that made a strange heaven out of unbelievable hell, and let's drink to the hope that one day this country of ours which we love so much will find dignity and greatness and peace again.

The play was clear in his mind, but he left the writing of it until the New York run of 'Private Lives' was over. That was not till the beginning of May and when he did begin, he found himself concerned as much as anything with the technical problems of insuring that there was never more than a thirty second pause between any of its three and twenty scenes. There was indeed on the first night a moment of terrifying suspense when the engineers reported that one of the lifts had stuck and that it would take two hours to repair it. Luckily the experts were, once again, at fault.

The rehearsals started in September. When my mother saw it she felt that she was seeing the whole of her life passing before her eyes. Everything was there. The troop-ship sailing to South Africa, the funeral of Queen Victoria, a young couple are making love on the boat-deck of a liner – a sudden searchlight plays on the liner's name. It is *Titanic*. There was Armistice Night in Piccadilly Circus. *The Times* critic called it, 'as comprehensive as Frith's Derby Day with an abounding vitality of its own.' In detail it was meticulously accurate. There was for instance, a scene in the East End in the summer of 1906. A newsboy carries a placard 'another Hayward century!' Only a small part of the audience would be likely to remember that in 1906, a summer of steady sunshine, Tom Hayward, the Surrey and England cricketer broke all records by compiling thirteen centuries, but for those who did remember, that unobtrusive placard gave the scene a vivid actuality. For other members of the audience, there must have been similar flashes of recall. It must have been obvious during the rehearsals that 'Cavalcade' was going to be a great success, but no one could have foreseen that its opening on October 12 would coincide with an almost hysterical wave of national enthusiasm.

After the first night's final curtain, Noël Coward said, 'I hope that this play has made you feel that in spite of the troublesome times we are living in, it is still pretty exciting to be English.' The King and Queen's presence on the second night set on it the imprimatur of Royal Benediction, like the State visit to a Cathedral to return thanks for a victory upon the battlefield.

In *Present Indicative* Noël Coward complains that it was regarded 'as a patriotic appeal rather than a play . . .' It was being distorted. He could, he wrote, have stayed on in England, and 'cashed in on all the tin-pot glory' but he felt it would be better for him to go abroad.

There have been so many financial crises since 1931, particularly since the second war, that it is difficult for any one now in his thirties to realise how intense a feeling of national rebirth there was during that autumn. It was very little less strong than the feeling of dedication that the country had after the evacuation at Dunkirk. People were so anxious to help their country that they lined up in queues to pay their taxes. Very stringent measures were adopted to meet the crisis. All official salaries were cut and no one grumbled. The sacrifices were made with pride. There was no feeling of gloom, of being reduced to sackcloth and ashes. There was an air of jubilation. In the autumn of 1940 J. B. Priestley in one of the Sunday night broadcasts that did so much to raise the country's spirits, said, 'If we have to live in a fortress, let us have fun in our fortress. Let us have the theatre, let us have music, let us have radio plays.'

There was the same spirit in England in the autumn of 1931.

During my three weeks at Chagford I had been conscious of this mounting exhilaration. I was acutely aware of it when I returned to my flat in Chelsea. There was a sense everywhere of homecoming, of wanderers returning, with everybody feeling, 'Well, now we are back here, we've done our duty. We've stopped taking pounds out of the country. We are going to "Buy British"; we are going to be economical. We are going to see how much fun we can have in our country, in our own homes.'

I got back from Chagford a week before Polling Day. The temper of the country can be gauged by the leaders in *The Times* and the political cartoons in *Punch*. Ramsay Macdonald was asking for a doctor's mandate, he was appealing to the country to be allowed to continue his work. There was a *Punch* cartoon for Everybody's Flag Day with the 'Buy British' slogan. The National Government was shown as the Protector of Britannia and her Lion. The Labour members who had refused to join Macdonald were shown as traitors, who had put their party before their country. The issue of *Punch* before the election had a 'Country First' cartoon. Macdonald was presenting the national party lion with the words, 'Let's see to it that he gets the Lion's share.' *The Times* on the eve of the election wrote, 'Never before has the British democracy been called upon to take a decision which in a single day will preserve or destroy the value of British currency and the solidity of British credit.'

Polling Day was on October 27. Never before has a Parliamentary party suffered a greater defeat than Labour did on that cold and foggy day. The National party was in with a majority of over five hundred. All the old Labour leaders were out, except Stafford Cripps. 'The country,' said *The Times*, 'delivered judgment in no uncertain terms on the men who ran away,' continuing, 'if only the National spirit which won it can be preserved then indeed the event of October 27 will give the nation such a chance as most people deemed impossible in mid-September.' My mother wrote jubilantly in her diary, 'wonderful return of National Government.' *Punch* in a cartoon called 'The Splendid Sword' showed John Bull by his anvil handing to Macdonald a sword marked 'national majority' and saying, 'The best job I've ever done, I feel sure that you can be trusted to use it well.'

The morale of the country touched its highest peak for thirteen years.

There was a corollary to this election of which few of us recognised the significance. It drove Sir Oswald Mosley into the wilderness. During the Spring he had launched his New Party and entered a dozen candidates for election. A weekly paper *Action* under the editorship of Harold Nicolson publicised his policies. Not one of his candidates was elected: the circulation of *Action* dropped from

165,000 copies a week to 16,000 a week and at the end of the year the publication was discontinued.

The story of the New Party has been told in Harold Nicolson's diaries and in Sir Oswald Mosley's autobiography. Mosley was unlucky; he not only lacked the gift of timeliness but time worked against him. At the very moment when he had planned to launch his party he was attacked by a combination of pleurisy and pneumonia, a very serious illness before the discovery of antibiotics. He could not be present at the opening meeting, and the Labour colleague whom he had relied upon to take his place, changed his mind at the last moment. During the early summer Winston Churchill was trying to enlist him under his banner as one of the 'Tough Tories'. He was still 'in the picture', but the financial crisis robbed his campaign of relevance. He was in fact in the position of 'ineffective isolation', against which his father-in-law warned him. 'Fate,' he said, in his autobiography 'confronted me with the dilemma of becoming a comfortable colleague in a journey to disaster or a lone challenger to a political world which was bringing ruin to my country.' He decided to found the British Union of Fascists on the German and Italian model, and eight years later was committed to gaol, without trial, as a potential menace to his country's safety.

His campaign ended in complete failure, but it was far from obvious during the 1930s that that would happen. England was very conscious of the Fascist danger. No one could be sure that a situation might not arrive when he and his lieutenants would seize power. It had happened in Italy and Germany. During the end of the decade it had appeared to be happening in Spain. His attacks on Communism made some people wonder whether Fascism might not be superior to Communism. He represented a danger of which Englishmen were conscious during the seven years before the outbreak of the second war; and all this started in the early winter of 1931.

XIII

The five weeks that I spent in London before and after the election were as good as any that I can remember. I did no writing. I was resolved to make up for my months of industrious absence and see as much of my friends as I could. One of the people I was most anxious to see was Betty Askwith. I asked her and Theodora Benson to a theatre, with Alan Pryce-Jones to meet them. We dined at my flat first. We went to Priestley's 'The Good Companions' returning to my flat afterwards, finding the fire still alive, banking it high with coal, and sitting in front of it on cushions. It was an evening that had for me a memorable and unexpected quality of charm. It is a misfortune for a man not to have a sister. It prevents him from meeting girls in a relaxed, family atmosphere. He meets only the girls with whom he is or is likely to become emotionally involved. A man who has a sister, sees girls about the place all the time; he sees them off parade. Berta Ruck told me that she could always recognise the man who had not had a sister. In addition to that in my case, an early and ill-fated marriage had cut me off from the debutantes I should have met had I been a young man about town in his early twenties. I had usually got involved with women a little older than myself. Either married women, or with the bohemian type that I met in Chelsea studios; Betty Askwith and Theodora Benson were almost the first two youngish girls – of what I suppose one has to call a society standing – whom I met on equal terms. Betty was to tell me later that that evening had a special quality for her too; it was the first time that she had been to a man's flat unchaperoned.

'I was surprised you were allowed to come,' I said. 'Was there any discussion?'

She shook her head. 'I suppose that my mother realised I was old enough to know what was right for me.'

It was the first time too, that I was to see Theodora in the company of a man by whom she was likely to find herself attracted. She and Alan Pryce-Jones found themselves on easy terms immediately. They laughed at the same things and when soon afterwards he needed to ask a female to lunch to meet my brother (not the easiest assignment) he chose her. She was quite different in Alan's company from what she had been with her conventional neighbours, from what she had been when I had tea with her and Betty, and also from what she had been at the *Lobster Quadrille* party where there had been no one 'special' for her. Her eyes were bright now and her voice had a wider range of tones. She was a highly delectable commodity. Betty, on the other hand, was very much the same, except that because she was having an amusing time, she was a little but only a very little more animated than she had been at the celebration party.

Alan and Theodora maintained the bulk of the conversation. They were both quick witted, they were both elegant and vibrant and they were having a good time throwing the ball back to one another. They were meeting for the first time; they were both thinking, 'Is this going to amount to something. It would be amusing if it did.' I let myself slide out of the conversation, letting myself try to picture the kind of life that lay ahead for these two girls. Both of them had been born under auspicious stars; the daughters of noblemen, they were not rich but they were to be spared many of the petty inconveniences that fret the existence of so many young women whose fathers have only what they earn, and who stand or fall by what they can make of their opportunities. Both were extremely talented. It was impossible to tell yet how talented or how strong the resolve would be to exploit those talents to the full. They were not ambitious, in the sense that they needed to push their way into the front; they were already in the front by birth. But the parable of the talents was real for them. They wanted to make the most of what they had.

How would it all work out? I could appreciate what a vivid, vivacious, many-coloured personality Theodora's was. She glittered on the surface. It was hard not to believe that she should be pursued by men; she had a giving nature. She might marry young, but if she did, it was hard to believe that she would remain rooted within one alliance. There would be lovers, there might be divorces. She had also been born at an unlucky time. The 20s was a period in which there was talk of 'superfluous women'. Norman Davey in 1923 published a novel, *Good Hunting* which he dedicated to the 2,341,207 superfluous women. For girls like Theodora and Betty the problem was that so many of the men from whom they could have taken their choice of husbands had been slaughtered on the Somme and at Paschendaele. There was a lack of men in their early thirties – the best age at that time for an English girl in her early twenties. It might well be that Theodora would not marry young; that she would have love affairs and marry late.

As it turned out, up to a point that was what did happen. She had many love affairs, but she did not marry.

At that time I knew nothing of her writing. I did not know how much of *Lobster Quadrille* was hers and how much was Betty's; but I had a suspicion that the lighter, the more flashing parts were hers. I presumed that before long they would acquire separate identities, that the divergent differences between them would grow more marked, that they would find it impossible to combine. I knew nothing either of Betty's writing. But I could sense that hers was a quieter, deeper nature. She had told me that she had written poetry. I fancied that as in writing she would be as different from Theodora in love. I did not think that she had the temperament for the *passade* as Theodora had: she would not make on the majority of men the instantaneous impression that Theodora was making now on Alan; but the men she did attract she would attract a lot. She would need a durable relationship. She would be looking for the man who could give her that. I remembered that swift flicker I had felt on our first meeting. 'You might be that man,' I told myself.

The weeks following the election which were supposed to be a time of solid retrenchment, were for me an animated period. It was over a year since I had spent any length of time in London. I was anxious to see the friends whom I had missed. My diary is dark with pencilled engagements for this and the other party. I had not yet taken up golf but I played squash two or three times a week to keep myself in training. A number of New Yorkers came across. Katherine Brush and her husband Bob Winans in particular. I gave a small dinner party for them. As Peters was still staying in my flat – he was planning to move into Albany and his set was not ready yet – I invited him to join us. 'Why not bring this new girl of yours.' I had not seen her yet, but I had not formed a favourable impression of her. One day when I was proposing to spend the night at Underhill, I had asked Peters if he would like to bring her to my flat. He was delighted and they shared my room which had a large double bed. On the bookshelves of the room were two photographs of females. I returned next morning to find the photographs placed face downwards on the mantelpiece. Not a courteous act. My first impression was confirmed during my dinner party. She was far from being unattractive. She was neat, trim, redhaired. But she was absolutely silent. She made no attempt to contribute to the evening's liveliness. 'I hope he doesn't marry her,' I thought. He did.

Somerset Maugham was over for a visit; as was his custom in the autumn. November is a bad month in the South of France. I had a very small party for him. Patrick Balfour, Marda Vanne who had acted in the English production of 'Rain', and Elizabeth Montagu, Lord Montagu of Beaulieu's daughter, who was making my heart beat a little faster at that time.

I took very good care to make the dinner a success. I was also on my guard. I knew how carefully Maugham would note each detail. At my dinner parties I invariably served champagne, both because I like it and because it 'makes a party go.' Spirits rise at the sight of a steaming bucket. But I suspected that Maugham knowing that I was very far from being affluent would think I was showing off. I decided therefore after consultation with my wine merchant to serve a heavy hock, fragrant, rich without being sweet. I cannot remember what my wine merchant suggested. I am puzzled by the nomenclature of German wines. I could pass an examination on paper, but I can never be really sure how the wine will taste. All I can remember about that wine, apart from its superb taste and bouquet, is that it cost fifty per cent more than the best current vintage champagne. There could be nothing ostentatious in serving a wine like that. If Mr Maugham did not know how good it was, then it was a sign of inadequacy in him. He made no comment on the wine; he was not the kind of guest who would, but Patrick, when I met him next, complimented me on its excellence. I recount this incident as an example of the self consciousness that Maugham induced in others – even in someone as unselfconscious as myself.

It was a pleasant party. Maugham was a better guest than he was a host. For him with his stammer parties were a strain. If he had produced a meal, he felt that he had made a sufficient contribution to the evening's gaiety. But when he accepted an invitation, he accepted an obligation to make the party go. I remember him asking me if I had ever read Carl Van Vechten's *The Tattooed Countess*. I said I hadn't. 'It's the best light comic novel I've read,' he said. He was to ask me the same question fourteen years later, when I was lunching with him and Carl Van Vechten in New York. Again I was to answer 'No.' Later I got the book and read it. It did not seem to me remarkable. I must try it again one day. If one does not like a book, it is as likely to be one's own fault as the author's.

Van Vechten had a strange career. He was highly successful as a novelist in the 1920s. *Peter Whiffle*, *The Blind Bow Boy*, *Nigger Heaven*, were good novels, and he was acclaimed critically. His sales were reasonably large, for the English market; he was, one of Grant Richards' discoveries. Then suddenly in 1932, he gave up writing and took up photography. He was a rich man. His name is engraved as a patron on one of the pillars in the hall of the New York Public Library. He could afford to indulge a hobby. He had said all he had to say. It showed a considerable amount of character to be able to quit the arena when his powers were still undrained. He appeared to be completely satisfied with his decision.

I recall many cosy parties during that November. Perhaps we Londoners felt that we had to concentrate a lot into that month, that it was a month of miracle that would not return, that for the moment we were all here together and that we must make the most of it. I remember, especially, a lunch at my flat when I introduced Newman Flower, the head of Cassell's, to my father. Just the three of us. It was a great success. Newman had never before met my father. He was in charge of a much larger firm. He was also quite a number of years younger than my father; I was midway between them. Newman was a West countryman, from Dorsetshire; with an accent that defied analysis, but that was real and rich. He was a great raconteur. He loved publishing and he loved authors. He was the only publisher I ever knew who did not, in estimating an author's value, work out whether or not that author had earned the advance that had been paid to him on account of royalties. He remembered the days when authors had sold their books to publishers for an outright sum. He would not think, 'I have paid Alec Waugh an advance of six hundred pounds on account of a twenty per cent royalty (in those days one got that kind of royalty). If he had sold 7,500 copies, he would have earned that advance, and I should have made £840. He has sold only 5,300 copies. He has not earned his advance, but even so I have made £535. I am well content with that.' On my first three novels, I did not earn my advance, but he did not lose money on me. Peters told me that he had a small black book, in which he had worked out the ratio of royalties to advances. He would consult this little book when the occasion for a new contract came up. 'Yes,' he would say, 'I can go on paying Alec the same advance.'

I had a very happy time with Cassell's for forty years. I was more than sad when they declined on moral grounds to publish my *A Spy in the Family*, I wished they could have stayed with me to the end. But in fact their adverse decision was a great piece of luck for me. Within a year the control of Cassell's had passed into other hands and Desmond Flower along with all the old directors left the board. I do not think I should have been happy with the new regime, though loyalty to the past would have prevented my leaving them. As it is, I have had extremely cordial relations with W. H. Allen who have issued a hard back edition of some of my early novels which I do not think Cassell's would have done.

John Farrar was also over. It was his first visit to England since the war, when he had passed through in uniform. The main object of his trip was to inveigle Remarque onto his list. Farrar and Rinehart had acquired *Cosmopolitan*, and Remarque had been a *Cosmopolitan* author. But Farrar also wanted to see his English authors, of whom he had a number, one of them being my brother Evelyn. I gave a small cocktail party for him. John Farrar still tells of that meeting with my brother. Farrar was seated on a sofa. I brought Evelyn up. 'This is your American publisher,' I said. 'Indeed,' he said, and bowed. He sat down and fixed on Farrar the stare that was to discountenance so many in the years ahead. It was intense. It was riveting. You were acutely conscious of the whites of his eyes. It completely deprived John Farrar of the power of speech. He stared back, hypnotised. They remained there, staring for what seemed an eternal Sargasso Sea of Silence; then Evelyn stood up, gave a little bow and walked away.

George Doran, who was John Farrar's literary godfather, was over in London too that autumn. It makes me feel very old to reflect that to hardly anyone under the age of fifty the name of George Doran can mean anything today. In the 1920s he was the Maecenas of the literary world as far as young English writers anxious to break into the American market were concerned. He was a Canadian, he loved England, and he specialised in English writers.

Before and during the war he built up Arnold Bennett, Somerset Maugham, and Frank Swinnerton. After the war he enlisted younger writers like Michael Arlen. His general view was if you acquired twenty promising English writers, even though you lost money on seventeen of them, it would not be very much and 'think what you could make out of the other three.' He believed in paying his authors rather more than they could expect to get anywhere else. He believed in giving a writer a sense of security and stability, of confidence in himself.

He always occupied the same suite at the Savoy high up looking out over the river – one of London's loveliest views. Its unostentatious luxury gave an author an encouraging feeling of being in good hands. Ethel Mannin in her *Impressions and*

Opinions – an autobiography that was in my opinion undeservedly attacked when it first appeared – gave an amusing account of a typical Doran party for his authors. I never had the good fortune to be in on one of those, but I was happy and proud to join his stable in the summer of 1926.

John Farrar had been trained in that Doran tradition. I remember well an occasion late in 1927, when I was passing through New York on my way back to London. I was at a low ebb emotionally and professionally. I was in the throes of a desperate romance for which I could see no hope; indeed there was none. And my last novel had done poorly in the U.S.A. It had not deserved to do much else, but it was my first novel with Doran, and I had hoped that the Doran salesmanship would lift it to respectable sales. It had actually done less well than had its predecessor with a smaller publisher. Would Doran want to go on with me? Was my American market in dissolution? I needed encouragement; and that was precisely what John Farrar gave me.

It took a little time, he said, for an English author to get known to an American audience. Moreover too many English writers were too English. 'But I have to use English subjects,' I remonstrated, 'I must write either about England or about Englishmen abroad. That's all I know.'

'Of course and that's what you should go on writing. There's nothing more phoney than the Englishman who writes about America as though he were American. But there's all the difference between that and the Englishman who spends a certain time in America, who has a number of American friends and who in consequence when he writes a story, automatically, without knowing that he's doing it, tells his stories in such a way that it will be comprehensible to Americans. If he absorbs the American point of view, he will find himself writing the kind of story that Americans want to read. I think you should come over and live here for a little.' Which was advice that I was to follow as soon as it became financially possible. 'Then you'll want to take my next book?' I asked.

'Of course, and the one after it.' I have never ceased to be grateful to John for saying that.

It is encouragement of that kind that an author needs from a publisher. He has so many moments of self-doubt. He needs to be reassured, to be told that everything is going well, and that very soon it will be going better. I never went to see my first publisher, Grant Richards, without coming away fortified. He looked so bland, so confident, so immaculately dressed. He was so unflurried. Everything seemed to be going well with him. Therefore since you were one of the things that were going with him, everything must be well with you. Later, I was to learn that affairs were very far from going well with him in the middle 20s. He was never secure financially. But he did not allow any of this uncertainty to show.

In November 1931 Doran was out of publishing. He had prudently sold out to Doubleday, when the going was good, and was over in London as W. R. Hearst's representative, commissioning English articles and stories for *Cosmopolitan*. Once again he was in a suite at the Savoy, and once again he was throwing a large party – this time a cocktail one for authors and prospective authors. It was hard to believe that English authorship was in a state of crisis when Hearst was ready to court it at such expense.

In spite of the crisis, a great deal of money was being spent in London. Undoubtedly the most striking party of the season is described in Michael Harrison's biography of Rosa Lewis. In talking about the bright young people whom my brother satirised in *Vile Bodies*, he sounds the requiem of their glory; he wrote:

The reign was over and we can give a day – 21.Nov.1931 – the day on which Arthur Jeffries, later a successful dealer in paintings, gave his famous Red and White party in Maud Allen's Regent's Park House. At this famous party at which Arthur wore white angola skin pyjamas, white elbow length kid gloves, ruby and diamond bracelets and carried a ruff of white narcissi, all the bright young things turned up, everyone in red and white. Evan Morgan was in a scarlet toga, his young gentleman friend was in a white ski suit with a white fur shako. Even the cigarettes were red as well as white, and only red and white things were there to eat. Lobster, strawberries, things like that. The late Brenda Dean-Paul, after having pulled a lady's hair for no reason except pure malice, was carted off by the police for being in unlawful possession of drugs. The late Hugh Walpole played 'Body and Soul' on the organ until Maud Allen in a rage sent down word that she had let the house not the organ and would they let her get some sleep. At seven in the morning they still weren't letting Miss Allen get some sleep.

I was invited to the party by Elizabeth Montagu. It started at about midnight. Elaborate security precautions were taken to ensure that there were no gate crashers. The cards of invitation were carefully scrutinised at the door. When the party started I was half-in-love with Elizabeth, by the time it ended I was three-quarters in love. I was unaware of the high drama that was being enacted round me. I was in a blissful haze. We sat around and held hands and drank very little, danced a little, talked to nobody except ourselves; until about five o'clock she drove me home. But I can see in retrospect that this party did mark the end of an era. As I said in my first chapter, 1931 was a watershed; a New World was to come into existence. There were to be no more parties like the airship one in *Vile Bodies*.

Early in December, so Michael Harrison reports, the *Bystander* delivered itself of an attack upon the party. 'How', it asked, 'could people not be expected to go communist when such ill-bred extravagance was flaunted, as hungry men were marching to London to get work.'

Many news items about Brenda Dean-Paul's addiction to drugs were to appear in the press during the next fifteen years. They were invariably illustrated by a photograph taken at the Red and White party. I scarcely knew Brenda Dean-Paul. In the middle twenties she was delightful company, witty, pretty and vivacious. It was cruel that that particular fate should have been decreed on her.

XIV

In the meantime the literary fortunes of the Waughs were progressing not unfavourably. Chapman & Hall's failing powers were a source of considerable concern to my father. At the moment when official salaries were being cut, R. E. Neale, the director who was appointed to watch the interests of the technical department – the story of his appointment in a palace revolution has been told in my *Early Years* – was suggesting a ten per cent cut in salaries for the staff and a fifteen per cent cut in directors' fees. The secretary, however, A. W. Gatfield, was demanding a rise of £100 a year. Ralph Straus resigned from the Board. The managing director, J. L. Bale, was in the full throes of a nervous breakdown. Early in October Curtis Brown told my father in the course of a lunch at the Devonshire Club that the Century Company of New York wanted to buy an English publishing house. It would no doubt have been in the interests of the shareholders, who had not received a dividend for many years, to have opened negotiations with the Century, but my father naturally did not want to organise himself into unemployment. After a perturbed Board meeting, Neale lunched my father at the Adelphi – a very sound hotel-pub whose bar was frequented by journalists. A four-course lunch consisting of mock turtle soup, fillet of sole, boiled beef and gorgonzola cost half-a-crown. The entry in my father's diary says, 'I had written a letter to Gatfield, but Neale urged me not to send it.' I would give a lot to know what was in that letter.

But in the meantime my father had the consolation of a very satisfactory reception of *The Road*. By mid-December it had sold 1,011 copies, which was a good sale for a book of that type and price; and *The Times* had included it in its list of the year's successes. He had every reason to be satisfied with its reception.

Evelyn's *Remote Peoples* appeared in late November. How quickly books were published in those days. He had not finished it when he was in Villefranche. As it was published by Duckworth and not Chapman & Hall there is no record of its sales in my father's diary. There is only one comment on it. 'Rebecca West "sniffy" about it in the *Daily Telegraph*.' I remember the review. It did not strike me as 'sniffy'. I should have been delighted to have been reviewed as warmly by Rebecca.

There are constant references to him however; entries that picture a disjointed life, as of course his was at that time. He had no home. He exiled himself on trips abroad. Then he would go into retreat and write. In the intervals he would, as it were, scurry from one pocket of resistance to another. In late October he went to Malvern to learn to ride. He was always conscious of his lack of height. He had, I fancy, an idea that his shortness would be less apparent when he was mounted. He did not persist with the experiment. He is recorded as having made Elizabeth Packenham – now Lady Longford – the nuptial presentation of a centenary Dickens. He lunches with Nancy Mitford, dines with Eleanor Smith, visits the Lygons at Madresfield, where he spent Christmas; always on the move.

My own novel, *So Lovers Dream* was published on November the 26th. I gave a small cocktail party for it. In those days, in England, it was unusual for publishers to give parties for their authors. Authors gave parties for themselves. On publication day I received from Newman Flower a letter written in his own hand, telling me how much he had enjoyed the book, congratulating me upon it. It did quite well. A favourable reception from the press and reasonable sales, a slight improvement on its predecessor. It did not earn its advance of six hundred pounds, but Cassell's did not lose money. Everyone was well content.

Two minor literary scandals stirred the world of letters in both of which John Farrar was concerned; in the one directly, the other indirectly. The indirect one was the case of Rosalind Wade's *Children Be Happy* – a novel about a girl's college life that was published by Gollancz. It was a good book and received good reviews. Rosalind Wade had been a friend of mine for several years. She had been secretary to Mrs Geoffrey Whitworth – whose husband was one of the directors of Chatto & Windus and herself was a lady of varied activities, one of which was the decoration of flats. She decorated my Chelsea one, and in the process I saw quite a little of Rosalind. I became very fond of her – a fondness that has survived. I also liked her book. I introduced her to John Farrar, throwing a small dinner which would give John the impression that she was a lady in good standing, as indeed she was. A useful author to have on the Farrar-Rinehart list. John succumbed to my persuasions and he acquired the American rights. The auguries were excellent. Unfortunately the book contained a minor character who mislaid her virginity. The character was identifiable, and the lady brought a libel action. In those days in England if a lady's honour was impugned you had not to prove special damage, as you would in a man's case. It might not do a military man any harm professionally to state that he had a mistress. A mistress after all was a status symbol of Ouida guardsmen, but such an imputation would damage the professional future of a cleric. To state that a woman was not a virgin, however, was to diminish her value in the marriage market. The character in Rosalind's book had only to satisfy the court that she was identifiable to demand damages. The judge took a very grave view of the whole affair. He awarded the plaintiff substantial damages: and ordered not only that every copy in existence but even the manuscript itself should be destroyed.

This happened forty years ago. Today a woman of twenty-three might claim that her matrimonial prospects had been damaged by the book that presented her, at that age, as a virgin.

It was cruel luck on Rosalind, and it says a great deal for her character and courage that she was not embittered by this experience. She went on steadily with her career and soon established a genuine reputation for herself.

The other scandal had greater repercussions because it involved Somerset Maugham. During the previous Spring, Farrar & Rinehart had been highly excited over a manuscript that they were to publish in the Spring called *Gin and Bitters*. Intended as a reposte to *Cakes and Ale*, it presented a novelist who was obviously Maugham travelling through the Far East, inveigling planters and officials into confidences that he was later to betray in print. There were reflections on his private life, though no suggestion of devious amatory tastes. But undeniably it held Maugham up 'to hatred, ridicule, and contempt.' The book was to be published anonymously, and there was a great deal of conjecture as to its authorship. Proofs of the early chapters were in circulation. It was obviously the work of a practised novelist; it had also been written by someone who had travelled in the Far East and the South Seas. As I was a Farrar & Rinehart author, it was suggested that I might be the author. John Farrar did not discourage the rumour. He wanted, naturally, to get the book talked about. The au revoir telegram that he sent me to the boat said, 'Who did write *Gin and Bitters?*'

When I eventually saw a complete copy of the book, I realised that it could only have been written by Elinor Mordaunt. I knew this because the anti-hero made a journey from Tahiti to Samoa. This was a very unusual journey, because Samoa and Tahiti are a long way apart, and there was no direct service between them; there was no reason why there should be: Tahiti was French, whereas Samoa, that had once been German, was now administered by New Zealand. Elinor Mordaunt had, however, made that trip and had told me about it proudly. It seemed to me most unlikely that any other writer would have made that trip, or that it would have occurred to another writer that such a trip was feasible. I had met Elinor Mordaunt once or twice at Gwen Otter's house and we had had a good time comparing travel experiences. I was never to see her again, so I had no chance of asking her why she had written *Gin and Bitters*. I was told that she had felt highly indignant over the portrayal of Thomas Hardy in *Cakes and Ale* and wanted to expose Maugham, in revenge. Maugham always denied that his Driffield was a portrait of Hardy, indeed there were very few resemblances. The course and conduct of their lives were completely different, yet I cannot believe that Maugham, while he was writing it, did not think 'some stupid people are going to mistake this for a caricature of Thomas Hardy.' There was the similarity of longevity, there was also the similarity between the shocked reception of Driffield's last novel and Hardy's *Jude the Obscure* which was reviewed as *Jude the Obscene*.

Gin and Bitters came out in the U.S.A. in the early summer. It did not sell very many copies, but it was discussed. Robin Maugham has described in *Somerset and All the Maughams* the avid curiosity with which it was received at the Villa Mauresque. Hugh Walpole made himself ridiculous – in view of the cruel picture of himself in *Cakes and Ale* – by delivering himself of a fierce attack on it. This inspired Will Dyson to draw a cartoon entitled 'The Noble Art of Self-Defence' which for many years hung in the Farrar & Rinehart office, and which was reproduced in my own *My Brother Evelyn and Other Portraits*. It showed a small frail woman holding a book before her face to protect herself from the assault of a man twice her size. Her assailant is unmistakably Hugh Walpole. The book in her hand is *Gin and Bitters*. The caption reads: 'Now no one can say that *Cakes and Ale* was meant for me.' In England the publication was eagerly awaited. It appeared in October under the title *Full Circle*. But the British enjoyment of its satire was short lived. Somerset Maugham moved in quickly with an injunction. He had no difficulty in persuading the court that the anti-hero was a picture of himself and that he had been held up to 'hatred, ridicule, and contempt' – the English definition of libel. The court in this case happened to be his brother, Mr Justice Maugham.

A day or two earlier John Farrar saw Somerset Maugham supping in the Savoy Grill. John had been one of Maugham's editors at Doran. He hurried over to him. 'Good evening Sir.' Maugham pointed a finger across the room. 'There is the door,' he said. And he did not stammer.

XV

Writers are often asked, 'How do you get the idea for a novel? Does it come to you in a flash?'

'Yes,' I answer, 'invariably. It is like falling in love at first sight.' Then I elaborate: I say 'sometimes a person is in love with love. He feels it is time he fell in love again. He goes to a party, looking for somebody. The result is never satisfactory. Love has to be spontaneous. It is the same with the writing of a novel. If I say to myself, "It is time I wrote a novel, the state of my finances decrees that I should write a novel. What shall I write about?" the book that results from this conscious effort never amounts to much. A novelist who depends on his pen for his livelihood does inevitably have every now and again to force himself to write a novel. And because he is a competent professional, he produces a readable commodity, but the writing of it is a weariness; and the book is soon out of print.'

When I returned to London shortly before the General Election, I had no working plans. I had two novels and a Benn's 9d. with publishers. I had also exhausted my store of short story plots. I would lie fallow for a while. But without warning, without willing it, the excitement of the hour germinated an idea. I wanted to express on paper the national enthusiasm that was pervading the entire country. I wanted to make myself, in my small way, the mouthpiece of the hour. I wanted to compare the depression as I had seen it in New York, with the economic crisis as I was living it in England. In the U.S.A. the stock market crash had weakened the American's faith in his country's destiny. In England the abandonment of the Gold Standard had restored the Englishman's belief in his country's future. From a distance of forty years, it may seem extraordinary that an Englishman should have been thinking that in 1931, but that was the temper of the hour.

It was a short lived hour. The period of disenchantment was swift to follow – the rising figure of unemployment, the despair that was expressed in the play 'Love on the Dole'; the sense that the economic structure of the capitalist world 'ailed from its prime foundation' when at a time that a large section of humanity was under-nourished, coffee was being burnt in Brazil and fish were tossed back into the sea, because they could not be marketed at a profit. Then was to come the pathetic panic-stricken appeasement of the dictators.

In retrospect the 1930s are seen as a period of shame for Britain. But in spite of that the autumn of 1931 was an hour of exultation. We were spared foreknowledge of what lay ahead, and I was in tune with the spirit of the hour when I devised a way of presenting that hour as the climax of post-war England in a book to be called *Thirteen Such Years*, which would show the transition of English life from the excitement of the Armistice celebrations to the General Election of 1931.

It would be told as a success story, a story that ended well, and it would not be difficult to organise. For the purpose of comparisons between London and New York I had the fifteen thousand words that on Eric Gillett's advice I had cut out of *So Lovers Dream*. I had moreover developed in earlier books such as *Myself When Young* a technique acquired from George Moore of weaving into the narrative short stories that were illustrative of a theme. I would, for example, be describing the position of the ex-officer now chained to an office desk and finding that the wife who welcomed his return each evening was a very less romantic object than the companion of his weekend leaves. I would then go on, 'I can best explain this problem by recounting the story of a certain brother officer of mine,' extracting from my files an appropriate story. Collections of short stories rarely sell, it is difficult to persuade a publisher to sponsor them, and this was a useful way of getting stories that I was fond of between covers. I had quite a number from which to take my choice. I should not probably need to write more than twenty-five thousand original words: less than three weeks. It was an occasion clearly for going into the country.

The obvious solution was a return to Chagford. But Elizabeth Montagu had invited me for a weekend to Beaulieu. I did not want to miss that; Chagford involved a full day's journey. Two years earlier I had gone to Margate to the Grand Hotel, where G. B. Stern was working on a play. I had enjoyed the comfort of a luxury hotel out of the season. The best rooms were at a minimum rate; there was an air of gilt and splendour about it all, and the air off the sea had a tonic quality. A six-day visit there would break the back of my book, then after the weekend at Beaulieu I could go back to Chagford and finish the book by Christmas.

The writing went easily at Margate. When the book appeared in the following summer, it had a better critical reception than I had received for quite a while. It was a serious book, and some critics had thought that my more recent novels had a playboy atmosphere. I made such good progress with the book that I felt I would be justified in spending four or five extra days in London before my return to Chagford.

I had been loath to leave London: it had become a new and exciting city for me. But somehow on my return, its atmosphere had changed. A current had been disconnected. I had during my last week declined a number of invitations. London is a city with a slow deep rhythm. When you once cut your threads, you have to start in all over again and adjust yourself to a new rhythm. I had nothing to do and with time hanging on my hands, I wondered how I would fare here during a bleak chill January. My flat was not centrally heated. It was on the river: damp mists would cling to its windows. I am slightly bronchial. I should have nothing to write. Betty Askwith and Elizabeth Montagu were powerful magnets: but a cautionary instinct counselled delay. I needed an interlude, a pause, to think things out; a January in London with myself at a loose end, no, that I was not ready for.

How though could I avoid it, when patriotic Britons were being adjured not to spend sterling in foreign countries? Europe and French colonies were out. New York was the best alternative. I should be taking sterling out of the country, but I would be bringing back to spend in England more dollars than I took out pounds. I could present my escape as a patriotic action. My travel agent informed me that the Olympic was due to sail on the 30th of December. I did not usually travel by such an expensive ship, customarily I took a French 9-day ship, the *de Grasse* or the *Lafayette*. So I booked myself second class and considered that the decline in my social status was a sacrifice endured for my King and Country. With my conscience clear and a ticket in my pocket, I went down to Chagford to finish *Thirteen Such Years*. I had not a trouble in the world.

I left for Chagford on December 12th, and the last days of 1931 were as good as any of those that had preceded them. Miraculously the weather held. The early mists dispersed and pale amber sunlight burnished the last shrivelling leaves. Eldred Curwen joined me; we went riding most afternoons: our feet grew cold in the stirrups; it was good to come back to tea before the fireplace, a tea with scones and Devonshire cream; then I would write for another ninety minutes before it was cocktail hour in Mrs Cobb's office-bedroom. After dinner we drove out to one or other of the pubs – usually to the Okehampton Arms, a fine sixteenth-century building that was run by a retired Colonel whose hobby it was to collect match boxes – a hobby that Evelyn gave to one of the characters in *Brideshead Revisited*. By eleven I was asleep, ready for my desk next morning.

I concluded the book with an imaginary character sketch of an English resident of the South of France: a man on the edge of sixty, who had been gassed in the first war and had carefully cherish his health in a kindly climate. When the country went off gold he considered it his duty to return to England.

'I've been thinking it out,' he said.

Until this crisis came along I never had. I'd always assumed things were all right. But when there came all that talk about the dole; and how the dole was responsible for the country's troubles, I began to think that it wasn't just a number of unemployed workmen who were on the dole; but the whole class of people like myself whom the country supports; because either they themselves or their parents at one time earned their country's gratitude. There are the retired colonels, and civil servants; and there are the people like myself who draw our incomes from the land because our ancestors earned and defended it. We're entitled to be supported. In the same way that an unemployed workman is entitled to be supported. But we're on the dole just the same. And in just the same way that an unemployed workman and a retired civil servant living abroad are a dead loss to their country, so am I. Every year for the last forty years the country has sent me three thousand pounds on which I've paid income-tax but which I have spent outside England. If I had died forty years ago the country would be a hundred thousand pounds better off. I had never thought of it in this way before. But when this trouble came I realised that England had too many responsibilities, that it couldn't afford to keep a whole host of people like myself upon the dole. But if I let my flat, brought back the rent of it and spent it along with the rest of my income here, well then, I should be no loss to my country. So I came back.

In my story, I made the return to London in November, a greater strain than his gas-weakened lungs could stand. When I read his obituary notice, I reflected he had given his life for his country, every bit as much as those of his contemporaries who fell at Ypres.

I finished the book on December 22 the day before Eldred and I were due to motor back to London.

The road led through Sherborne. We reached there shortly after twelve. 'Why don't we lunch here?' Eldred asked. I shook my head. I had still not made my peace with Sherborne. I was not a member of the Old Boys' Society. If I had gone to the tap-room of Old Tom Bowley's, I might have met one of the masters. 'What do you think he'd do to you if you did?' said Eldred. But I was not to be tempted. Not only would it be in the worst of taste, but I regarded it as a privilege that I to whom Sherborne meant so much, should be the one person in the world who could not drive up its main street, stop at the Castle Arms and order a pint of beer. I remembered how Swann had regarded it as a privilege that he could not go to the village where Odette was staying. Everyone else in the world could go there. Indeed the railway company made it easy for anyone to go there by publishing time-tables of its trains. He alone could not avail himself of their facilities. So we did not stop at Sherborne and followed the main road to Salisbury.

We had brought up with us a Christmas Turkey, it was to prove something of what my Norton aunts used to call, a 'worry-joy' for it had not been plucked or eviscerated, but by the time it emerged from the oven, it was manifestly a noble beast.

We had a quiet Christmas. The only other guest was E. V. Lucas's daughter, Audrey Scott. Her father and mine had been great friends and the tradition had grown up, I do not quite know how, that she should have Christmas dinner with us. Eldred and I had arranged to pick her up. In the afternoon we decided to have a Turkish Bath. Selfridge's Information Bureau informed us that the Turkish Baths in the Imperial Hotel in Russell Square were open. To our astonishment we found that it was crowded with a group of Jews who came here every Christmas afternoon. They all knew each other. They were having a wonderful time, shouting, joking, smoking cigarettes in the hot rooms. There were twenty of them to one masseur, but Eldred and I had no difficulty in getting proper attention. None of the others seemed to want a massage. They were making a party of it.

An interviewer asked me once what I most enjoyed about travelling. 'The arrivals and departures,' I replied. And I think I enjoy the departures most, particularly the drama of the goodbye party, with the knowledge that one will be on the high seas next day, while all these others will be continuing their habitual routine. I had my goodbye party in my flat. There were Theodora Benson, Betty Askwith, Elizabeth Montagu, a girl friend of Eldred's; there must have been two other men. I cannot remember who. We had a couple of boxes for a Christmas Pantomime at the Chelsea Palace. It was a pleasant, but not a hilarious party.

Next morning I caught an 8.00 A.M. train from Waterloo. Both Theodora and Elizabeth came to see me off. I was a little annoyed at seeing Theodora there. I suppose she had come in support of Betty's interests. I had hoped to have a word with Elizabeth. But perhaps, I reflected, as I took my last look at the Thames, it was as well that Theodora was there. Eight o'clock on a station platform in December is not the time for sentiment. I might be now regretting what I had said or failed to say. Better not to have had a chance of saying anything.

Three years earlier I had made a winter crossing on the *Berengaria*. The ship had been crowded, but that was when the stock market was riding high. Today there were only seventy first class passengers, and I had to myself a large cabin with a bath, that in the season was included in the first class accommodation. The second class dining room was only a third full. One table apart from the others was occupied by a dozen elegant men, wearing black coats, stiff white collars and striped trousers. They were the valets – the gentlemen's gentlemen – of certain exclusive first class passengers. The ship was so empty that among the second class passengers was Captain Knight – the owner of the Golden Eagle – on his way to a lecture tour. He had been travelling on the *Berengaria* three years ago. But then, like me, he had been travelling first class.

Another second class passenger who usually I imagine travelled first class, was Sylvia Thompson. She also was going for a lecture tour. She was about to publish a novel called *Summer's Night*. Its title had been taken from the same quotation as mine had

So Lovers dream a rich and rare delight

And get a winter seeming summer's night.

I had met her once or twice, but this was the first time I had had a chance of a real talk with her. This trip was the start of a friendship that I was to value greatly. I wonder if any of her books are still in print? I question it. Old books have to make way for new ones. I recently asked Desmond Flower how many of Arnold Bennett's books, in addition to *The Old Wives' Tale* were still in print. 'Only two, *Riceyman Steps* and *Imperial Palace*. It would probably pay us to reissue at least *Lord Raingo*, but even as big a firm as ours can only handle a certain amount of titles, and we have to give new writers the best chance we can.'

Naturally readers prefer contemporary stories, with which they can identify themselves. Problems of love are different today when you can hop a plane and 'find out what the hell's the matter', from what they were in 1930 when a business executive could not take the time off to cross the Atlantic and sort out a personal issue; as

189

happened for instance in Marcia Davenport's *Her Constant Image*.
Sylvia Thompson's novels might well seem dated now. But they
had very real qualities. One of the chief being the sense you had,
that the author herself was someone very likeable.

I never saw her after the war. She ceased writing early, and I
have wondered why. Between 1937 and 1939 under Carl Brandt's
guidance and encouragement, she concentrated upon short stories.
She did a number of excellent ones, which sold to high paying
magazines. Did she find it difficult to work for the American
market, with the uncrossable Atlantic in between? Did she take
on war work of some kind and find herself unable to get back to
writing afterwards? She became a Roman Catholic. Did this
change of faith make her feel that writing for magazines was
trivial? I kept meaning to try to get in touch with her. But
somehow communications were difficult in the England of the
50s, and as a foreign resident I was in England less than three
months a year. I felt guilt as well as regret when I read of her
death in 1965. She was a rich rare person.

There must have been festivities of some kind on New Year's Eve,
but I took no part in them. Dinner in the second class was early.
The clock had gone back an hour and midnight was one o'clock to
me. I was asleep by ten o'clock. No doubt over a solitary nightcap,
I took an inventory of the year that was about to end. No doubt,
I thought, gratefully that it had been pretty good all things considered – not a great deal on the debit side of the ledger. But I
should have been very surprised could I have known that in
forty-three years' time I should be writing about it as, 'the year I
would soonest relive.'

The leader writer of *The Times* was describing it as 'a black
year in the history of the world' though he added the consolation
that 'for Great Britain and the Empire as for the U.S.A. it has
been a year of awakening'.

In Hampstead my father was writing the last entry in his diary.
'So ended my second year from the office of which let me re-
member chiefly its blessings. Much kindness at home and abroad.
Particularly from K and Alec. A happy month at Villefranche

which probably saved my life and an unexpectedly good reception for my book. The last two months have been full of kind letters about it which have done much to comfort me in anxieties of business and finance. And K and I have been very happy together, although I hate to see her slave so hard in the house. If only we could sell Underhill in the spring, the future would not look so dark. At any rate we must keep up our hearts. We have endured worse things.'